FAIR GAME

A Complete Book of Soccer for Women

LORRIE FAIR with **Mark Gola**

Foreword by Anson Dorrance
University of North Carolina women's soccer head coach

A Mountain Lion Book

Contemporary Books

Chicago   New York   San Francisco   Lisbon   London   Madrid   Mexico City
Milan   New Delhi   San Juan   Seoul   Singapore   Sydney   Toronto

Library of Congress Cataloging-in-Publication Data

Fair, Lorrie.
    Fair game : a complete book of soccer for women / Lorrie Fair with Mark Gola.
        p.   cm.
    Includes index.
    ISBN 0-07-139095-2
    1. Soccer for women.   2. Fair, Lorrie.   I. Gola, Mark.   II. Title.

    GV944.5 .F35   2003
    796.334'082—dc21   2002031416

To the memory of my father,
Bennett Cooper Fair Jr.,
and to the most competitive, logical,
loyal, loving, supportive, and by far
the silliest people on earth:
Thanks, Mom, Greg, Ronnie,
Pooh, and Uncle Robear
LMF

1 2 3 4 5 6 7 8 9 0   QPD/QPD   2 1 0 9 8 7 6 5 4 3

ISBN 0-07-139095-2

Interior photographs by Mike Plunkett

The Philadelphia Charge logo is a registered trademark of the Women's United Soccer Association and is used in this book with permission of the WUSA.

McGraw-Hill books are available at special quantity discounts to use as premiums and sales promotions, or for use in corporate training programs. For more information, please write to the Director of Special Sales, Professional Publishing, McGraw-Hill, Two Penn Plaza, New York, NY 10121-2298. Or contact your local bookstore.

This book is printed on acid-free paper.

Contents

Foreword

I can still remember the first time I saw Lorrie Fair play. I was recruiting for the University of North Carolina at Chapel Hill when I watched Lorrie in an all-star/ODP (Olympic Development Program) game between northern California and southern California. Even back then she had such a clean technique and she worked hard. She scored a beautiful goal, but the thing that sold me on her was not the goal but how tenaciously she tracked on defense, even though she was playing as a striker the entire game. I knew from just that one game that Lorrie was going to be a special player. I just hoped there was a chance to have her become a special player for me at UNC.

Usually, a player grows on you during the recruiting process. There are so many extraordinary players out there, so it can take several evaluations to place where she would fit in your recruiting class and where she would be recruited to fit on the field. The University only permits me to recruit four out-of-state players a year, so when I recruit someone I can't make a mistake—she *has* to play. I knew instantly that Lorrie could play anywhere in the country and anywhere on the field, but our team's holes at the time were in the back and in the midfield, so it was a bit unnerving to share in my first recruiting call to Lorrie that, yes, UNC would love to have her, but we were not going to look at her to strike. Much to my relief Lorrie did not cross us off her list when I told her we were looking to change her position.

I learned many things about Lorrie during recruitment. From our first conversation to our last, she was a pleasure to speak to on the phone. Her talented twin sister, Ronnie, was also fun to catch up with, and even though we were not recruiting her she was someone I looked forward to talking to whenever I called. I developed a great affection early on for Lorrie's mom, May, who since the death of Lorrie's father years ago was raising her son and two daughters by herself—no easy feat with the high energy of those three.

Many things have drawn me close to Lorrie over the years, but the first time she wowed me was at the end of the recruiting process. Like every other Division I program out there, UNC has a roster that is larger than its scholarship allocation. And though we actively recruit very few athletes, we had run out of scholarship money by the time Lorrie had decided where she wanted to go to school.

I thought our last conversation on the phone was on the day before she was to join Tony DiCicco in a training camp for the full national team, an amazing honor for an athlete still in high school. She decided she wanted to "commit" before she left for camp. I wanted her to come to UNC in the worst way, but I did not have a dime for her for her first year. She had wonderful offers from many elite schools and programs, and, given that her mother would have to put her two other siblings through school at the same time as Lorrie, we had a tearful phone call when she shared she could not afford to come. I phoned Bill Palladino, my long-time top assistant and friend, to tell him Lorrie was not coming and called it an evening. Because I make my recruiting calls from my office I locked up and went home. This was a west-coast call and a three-hour time difference for me, so it was pretty late when I got home. As I began to explain to my wife, M'Liss, about how I had just lost an amazing player and a wonderful human being, the phone rang.

"I'm coming!"

"What?"

"I'm coming to UNC!"

"You're kidding me!"

May Fair could see where her daughter's heart was, and she was going to sacrifice everything to support her daughter in this decision.

The rest, as they say, is history. Lorrie's career at UNC was everything we both had dreamed. She could play everywhere and she did. Every year she kept getting better, winning national championships and ascending to the most celebrated U.S. national team roster . . . the 1999 team . . . world champions in front of 90,000 in the Rose Bowl. In that championship, she played for a period in every line: up front, in midfield, and in the back—the only player to do so. *And* she was the youngest player on the roster.

Flush from her World Championship triumph, she was again in the throes of a dilemma. Each world championship athlete was to receive a monetary bonus and an equally lucrative "Victory Tour" paycheck. No one would have thought any less of her if she were to withdraw from her final year of collegiate eligibility to chase this earned opportunity and graduate with this wonderful nest egg.

I will never forget what she told me when she decided to return to play her senior year, virtually giving away a huge bonus check and "Tour" paycheck to keep her amateur status and play for UNC one last season.

"Anson, I have some unfinished business here, and I want to graduate a national champion."

You see, Lorrie had won national championships her freshman and sophomore seasons. But our team was runner-up her junior year, and she wanted to come back and help us win it back. And she did.

Like for the U.S. national team in 1999, Lorrie Fair was all over the field in 2000. The first part of the season she was in the middle of midfield; then when we struggled to score, we threw her up top, and then when we knew we needed her in the back to help bring the championship back to Chapel Hill, she sacrificed her love for playing in the midfield and played in the back for us. In one of the best-organized defenses in the history of our program, Lorrie sacrificed everything: the money and the position she most enjoyed playing to help deliver us back to number one.

That year, she won a national player of the year award to cap a brilliant collegiate career. But it is not over for Lorrie Fair. She continues to get better. Her underrated team, the Philadelphia Charge, baffled critics by overachieving its first year and making the playoffs. The ascension continued the second year as the Charge dominate most of the season only to be eliminated by the Washington Freedom, just missing the Founders Cup once again.

I was honored when Lorrie asked me to be among the first to read this book. She takes you on a personal tour of this great game, and as only one of soccer's finest young technicians can, Lorrie illustrates how much fun playing has been for her thus far and how you can have fun too. Although she takes what she does seriously, she does not take herself seriously, and her love of the game and her fun-loving personality shine throughout. You will enjoy every page.

Anson Dorrance
University of North Carolina
women's soccer head coach

Preface

When my twin sister, Ronnie, and I were growing up, my father would sign us up for any sport we expressed interest in playing. Whether it was basketball, baseball, volleyball, track, or soccer, my dad would register us in the league, get us on a team, and then volunteer to coach.

My dad wasn't a great athlete, nor was he a sports connoisseur. In fact, he probably didn't even know enough about the sport to coach, but he was always eager to show enthusiasm toward his children wanting to participate in athletics. So what would he do? He would buy the book.

My father was notorious for acquiring books from the library or bookstore and reading about the fundamentals of a sport he was about to coach. He would absorb information through written word and then impart it to those he would guide. He may never be mentioned with the likes of Vince Lombardi, Phil Jackson, Pat Summit, or Anson Dorrance, but he was perfect for youth sports. His intent was to teach kids, improve their skills, make sure they respected the game, and, above all, have fun.

I'd like to think that *Fair Game: A Complete Book of Soccer for Women* would be the crown jewel of my father's book collection. Like so many other aspects of my life, his memory inspires me to achieve the best, and this book is a tribute to what he's meant to me throughout my life. Of course, it helped to be a twin, a younger sister, a best friend, and a daughter to the most incredible people in my life. My family and friends are a huge part of my life, and you will get that feeling immediately as you read the personal anecdotes.

Fair Game is not your typical soccer instructional book. It outlines (in detail) the fundamental skills of the game and how to execute them, but within each chapter are my personal experiences from playing for the U.S. women's national soccer team, the U.S. Olympic team, the heralded University of North Carolina women's soccer dynasty, and the Philadelphia Charge of the newly formed Women's United Soccer Association (WUSA). Personal anecdotes and comments from family, friends, and teammates interwoven throughout give each chapter life and sometimes comedy. Accounts of playing in front of ninety thousand fans during the 1999 World Cup title game, winning the under-16 (U-16) national championship with my club team (the Sunnyvale Roadrunners), claiming three NCAA national titles at UNC, and playing alongside world-class players such as Julie Foudy, Tiffeny Milbrett, Michelle Akers, and Mia Hamm add fuel to fire in the upcoming pages. What I've been able to experience in the sport of soccer has been far beyond my wildest dreams, but believe me, it can happen to you, too.

The information in this book is presented in an entertaining and easy-to-read format that will provide you with knowledge and advice in all facets of the game. The first chapter, "It Takes More Than Talent," describes the attributes beyond foot skills that are integral to developing into a quality player. Elements such as playing with heart, finding motivation, using positive imagery, and dealing with failure are featured. The chapter's ideas can be extended beyond the soccer field to any aspect of life. Chapter 2, "Rules and Equipment," supplies the reader with the game's guidelines but also introduces what it means to put on a uniform, the intricacies of playing on different surfaces, and how to and how not to talk to referees.

Chapters 3 through 8 cover the basic skills of the game: dribbling, passing, receiving, shooting, goalkeeping, and heading. These are the core instructional chapters and must be read attentively because each one branches into how to apply the specific skills in competition. For example, Chapter 3 reviews the rudimentary skills of dribbling, but also discusses when to dribble, when not to dribble, how dribbling can be used strategically to break down defenses, and, of course, advanced dribbling moves.

Game strategy becomes increasingly vital as you advance to higher levels of play. In playing for UNC, the U.S. women's national team, and the Philadelphia Charge, I've competed in a variety of formations amid an assortment of team philosophies. I'll examine each team's strategy and suggest how your team should approach the game when considering your strengths and weaknesses.

Restarts, which can have a tremendous impact on the outcome of a game, are explored in Chapter 10, followed by the conditioning chapter. You might have the greatest technical skill in your league, but you must be in playing shape to execute those skills throughout an entire game. Topics like balance, agility training, proper rest, and nutrition are presented and explained.

The final chapter, "The Life," gives you an insider's look at what it's like to be a professional athlete. I'll talk about all the countries I've visited, having an agent, endorsement contracts, making special appearances, and even how I handle having a bad day. While my first priority is always soccer, I've experienced a lot of great things off the field, such as going to the Super Bowl the past three years courtesy of Gatorade. But all of these things have happened to me because of the game and the wonderful people who are in its circle.

After you've finished reading this book, I can guarantee you several things. You will definitely laugh, you will get to know me like your neighbor, you'll learn about my family and friends, and most important, you'll become a better soccer player. This book is packed with tips and advice on understanding the nuances of the game, how to refine your skills, how to apply those skills to the field of play, and how to think like a winner.

My father learned the game of soccer from reading books and applying what he learned to those he coached on the playing field. I hope *Fair Game* will have the same positive influence on you that my father, family, and friends have had on me. Best of luck achieving your aspirations in soccer and life, and enjoy the book!

Lorrie Fair

Acknowledgments

This book was conceived, developed, and produced by Mountain Lion, Inc., a book producer specializing in instructional and general reference sports books. A book producer relies on the specific skills of many people who contribute their talent and efforts. To all of them we'd like to say, "Thanks":

Rob Taylor and Michele Pezzuti at Contemporary Books/McGraw-Hill, for belief and support of this project.

Michael Plunkett, photographer, who took all the instructional and game-action photographs for the book.

Anson Dorrance, legendary women's soccer coach at the University of North Carolina, who wrote the foreword.

Margaret Trejo, who created the diagrams.

Dave Bober and Marla Mullen of Octagon, who encouraged Lorrie Fair to write her story.

Jenny Benson, Heather Mitts, Mandy Clemens, Karen Hall, Mary Francis-Monroe, Janel Schilling, and Stacey Tullock, who were models in the photo shoot and helped on their day off.

Villanova University women's soccer head coach Ann Clifton for use of the field and to the facilities staff who prepared the field for the photo shoot.

Greg Wiley, director of public relations for the Philadelphia Charge.

Greg Smith at Nike, who supplied Nike apparel for the photo shoot.

Also, May Fair, Ronnie Fair, Greg Fair, Jennifer "Pooh" Medina, Anson Dorrance, April Heinrichs, Tony DiCicco, Mia Hamm, and Julie Foudy for giving us their time to be interviewed and the entertaining comments they provided.

A special thanks from Mark Gola to Edward F. Gola, Gary Vogler, Edward McManimon, Warren Maruca, Don Busch, and Stan Davis for their time and commitment to teaching youths the great game of soccer. And, of course, a special thanks to Lorrie Fair.

"When I'm on the soccer field,

I play with my heart, body, and mind."

It Takes More Than Talent

People ask me all the time, "How did you get to where you are today?" If I had a secret or a simple answer, believe me, I would share it with every young girl who plays soccer. I sometimes scratch my head when I think of all the great things I've experienced playing this game, and the many more that lie ahead. I never imagined playing for the under-16 (U-16) national championship with the Sunnyvale Roadrunners, never thought that I'd receive an athletic scholarship to play soccer at the University of North Carolina (UNC), never expected to be a member of the U.S. women's national soccer team, and never in my wildest dreams did I think I'd earn my living playing in a women's professional soccer league. I've traveled to dozens of countries, met and befriended people of all different walks of life, and even appeared on an episode of MTV's "Real World/Road Rules Challenge." Soccer doesn't necessarily define me, but it's been the epicenter of my growth and development as a person.

No prescribed formula allows people to accomplish their life's goals. I attribute my achievements to athletic ability, a bit of good fortune, and sheer passion for the game. It's truly an amalgam of elements that have blended into a healthy solid. But one absolute that I can tell you is this: playing soccer entails a lot more than fancy dribbling, well-timed through passes, and precision shooting. Soccer takes more than talent.

There are girls out there who are bigger, stronger, and faster than I am. There are players who possess harder shots, better moves, and superior leaping ability. To compete and persevere, I have to tap into all of my resources. When I'm on the soccer field, I play with my heart, body, and mind.

Passion

I specifically mentioned passion because it's played such a vital role in my development as a player. Passion is the difference between wanting something and actually going and getting it. You can want to be good at something, but if you have passion for it, it electrifies the effort

Fair is Fair

When Ronnie and I began playing competitive soccer, we honestly went out and played to have fun. There was never any master plan. We didn't join a club team in hopes of gaining exposure and moving onto the Olympic Development Program or playing in front of college recruiters. In fact, when we first joined the Sunnyvale Roadrunners, our team didn't exactly set the world on fire. We improved through growth and experience and eventually won the U-16 national championship. Things just happened as I progressed, but my intentions were always pure. My desire to play augmented my talent, and without that desire, I wouldn't be playing today for the Philadelphia Charge, the U.S. women's national team, or anywhere else for that matter.

I do not recommend joining club teams and traveling to elite soccer tournaments and camps with expectations of gaining fame or popularity. You'd better be out there because you love playing the sport. Club soccer is a huge time commitment, and if you're participating only because of your parents or friends, you'd better take a step back and reevaluate your situation. Your years of youth are sacred. Enjoy your time doing what you want. If that is playing soccer, then great! But don't play because of outside pressures. Live your life for your own enjoyment.

put forth to achieve your goals. I think that applies to everything in life, not just sports.

My passion for soccer developed immediately. I played almost every sport but loved soccer most out of them all. I discovered that I was athletic when I was young and enjoyed succeeding as an athlete. I wanted to get better because I was having so much fun being good at something. I think everyone—kids, teenagers, and adults—enjoy doing things they're good at. I found I was good at soccer. All I wanted was the ball so I could just take off with it.

In youth leagues, I scored a lot of goals and wreaked havoc all over the place. My twin sister, Ronnie, and I were two of the better players out there, and that was all the satisfaction we needed. I never thought about soccer being a ticket to college or an opportunity to travel and play with select teams. I played because I loved it and embraced competition.

The Ireland family ran a soccer academy right near our house. Vick Ireland was the father and he had three sons—Simon, Gary, and Ross. They had all played professional soccer and became coaches at the academy. Ronnie and I would go over there everyday and knock on their office door, trying to pull them out of their chairs to play. Now mind you, we were twelve years old and they were men in their early twenties. They'd see us coming down the street and think, "Oh no. Here they come again." But they would always play with us, whether it was in the office or on the field across the street. We were like little runts running around and they'd shove us around a bit, but as we grew up and improved, they had to start playing a little more seriously. Once we started hitting back, the gloves were off.

Now we go out there and play all out. It's great to stay in contact with those guys, because they really helped my development as a player. I saw how good they were and wanted to be better.

My passion for the game is really what has driven me to success. It's sometimes hard for me to talk or even write about soccer. I just want to play! That feeling is still the same for me now as it was when I was nine years old—that love for the game. And I tell everybody, as soon as I lose that desire to play, I'm hanging up the boots. Whether I'm at the top of my game or the bottom, if I lose the desire to play, that unequivocal passion, it's time to do something else.

Heart

Your heart is the one thing you can always count on. Some days, your touch is not always perfect, your timing might be off, or your brain is having trouble focusing. Like it or not, even the very best athletes have bad days. But you can always rely on your heart no matter how poor your execution might be.

To play the game with heart means that you give everything that you possibly can. You have nothing left to give to the game or your teammates. That's the way I felt after playing the 2000 Olympic final game in Sydney, Australia.

I'm very, very proud of the silver medal that we won in 2000. Part of me hurts because I feel like we outplayed Norway in that gold medal game. That's a lesson you'll learn in soccer and life. Sometimes, the ball doesn't bounce your way, and the outcome can favor a team that was beaten on the field. But personally, I know deep down that there was absolutely nothing else that I could have given on the field that day. It just wasn't meant to be. I'll just use the experience to motivate me even more for the 2004 Olympics. Regardless, it's pretty cool to own an Olympic silver medal.

Playing with heart can make a difference in winning tackles, headball, and 50/50 loose balls (balls that can be won by either team). It's a resource that can push you over the edge in achieving a favorable outcome.

When the 1999 World Cup final is mentioned, most people will talk about the shootout and Brandi Chastain's final kick. Do you know what *we* often talk about? We talk about nearly losing that game by four inches in overtime. That four inches was Kristine Lilly's forehead, which was what she used when she leaped up and headed a ball off the goal line on a corner kick that was destined for the back of the net. Without her being in that spot and making the effort to go up and get that ball, that shootout would have never even happened. Kristine's game-saving header was just as

There is no greater feeling than knowing you are the best soccer team in the world.

important to that World Cup title as any of those penalty kicks.

To influence a game, sometimes all it takes is a toenail—that extra reach to keep a ball in bounds and maintain an attack. Colleen Hacker, our sports psychologist on the national team, told us about a five-hundred-lap car race that was won by an inch. Some minuscule occurrence, maybe even something in the pit stop that delayed the car for an instant, was the difference between winning and losing that race. So everything you do in a game, whether it's scoring the game-winning goal or barely getting a toenail on the ball to deflect it to one of your teammates, can influence the outcome. Every effort you make can become the determining factor.

It's Fair to say . . .

Have you ever fast-forwarded through a video? That's what eating dinner looked like at my house growing up. There wasn't always enough for everyone to have seconds, so it was a frantic race to see who could earn the second helping. There was very little conversation, mostly just scooping and shoveling.

We used to make fun of Ronnie because she was always the slowest eater. My brother could scarf down food at incredible speeds, and I'm no slouch myself, but Ronnie would always finish a few bites behind.

When Ronnie went to college at Stanford University, she called me up at Carolina and was all excited. "I'm not a slow eater!" she yelled out. "It's only by our family's deranged standards that I'm slow. I finish dinner first here at school."

Perhaps girls consciously eat slower to avoid looking like they're "pigging out." But in my family, being a fast eater is like wearing a badge of honor. In all honesty, I'm working on eating a little slower, but sometimes, old habits die hard.

Competitiveness

There is absolutely nothing wrong with wanting to be the best. You owe it to yourself. With all the time and hard work you put in, why would you seek anything less? A strong, competitive attitude is healthy, and it is evident in those who are successful in all aspects of life.

Growing up with a twin sister certainly helped stimulate my competitive nature. It was always, "Who's taller now?" "Who is better at this?" "Who got the higher grade on the test?" Throw my older brother, Greg, into the mix and our household was like a twenty-four-hour event. The dinner table was a popular forum

for epic battles in my family. We'd have staring contests, laughing contests, we'd race to see who could eat the fastest. It was insanity.

To me, being competitive isn't simply about loving to win and hating to lose. Everyone likes to win and no one likes to lose. That's human nature. I think being competitive is a matter of wanting to perform at your very best all the time, to elevate your level of play to the highest possible standards. That's why great athletes flourish against great competition. They love the challenge because it brings out the best in them.

When I started being asked to try out for select teams, I realized how much I loved competing. There were girls who had been on select teams in previous years, so I had an "everything to gain and nothing to lose" type attitude. I was never intimidated but instead was eager to see how I'd measure up against more established players. As it turned out, they brought out the best in me. Playing with and against better players raised my level of play and accelerated my progress.

Competing Among Teammates

Being competitive among your teammates is something that girls have a hard time with. The word *competitive* can even take on a negative connotation. I think that belief starts when you're young. In grade school, the boys will go out and play kickball, basketball, or "kill the pill." They're always trying to beat one another at some competition. The girls won't play a game like that. They'll play something that involves everyone participating in unison, where there's no winner or loser, such as ring-around-a-rosy.

I think males and females grow up under a different set of rules—a different set of standards. And competitive sports are not conducive to those preconceived beliefs of how a female should act individually and among her peers. Slowly but surely, we're breaking down those barriers. Girls have to understand that competition is a part of life. You've got to separate yourself from that girl you are in the classroom or at the mall from the girl you are on the playing field. Maintain your respect for people, but during competition, it's not the time or place to make buddies. Just make sure everything gets left on the field. Don't take up those issues off the field because playing hard positively influences your game. One of the reasons competition is perceived as negative is because people bring their negative emotions off the field.

I really had an advantage in having siblings who competed with each other. Greg, Ronnie, and I would go at it all the time. My parents would never interfere, which sent us the message that it was okay to compete. At the end of the day, we all still loved each other, despite the bumps and bruises.

We had that type of atmosphere at the University of North Carolina. I'd come home more banged up and exhausted from practice than I did from games. We went at each other pretty hard, but the moment we'd step off the field, all was forgotten. It's understood that playing hard and aggressively in practice benefits yourself, your teammates, and the team.

During the inaugural season in the WUSA, I would get this question all the time. "What's it like playing against all your teammates on the national team?" To be honest, I go harder against my teammates. If I don't, they'll get the best of me because I know they're going to go harder at me. It's a sign of respect for one another.

When you go out on the field, whether it is to practice or play a game, everyone has agreed to compete. Some might argue that competition is negative and creates bad feelings. In my opin-

My mom; my brother, Greg; my sister, Ronnie; and me. We get along great, as long as there is plenty of food to go around at the dinner table.

ion, competition doesn't create bad feelings, people do. Girls need to learn that it's okay to compete.

Motivation

One characteristic that all great athletes have in common is that they're motivated. What makes individuals unique, however, is their source of motivation. It doesn't matter where it comes from, it simply needs to be evident in your approach to the game.

Motivation is something that has to come from within. It can't be manufactured by the impending will of an outside source. For example, I've seen parents put way too much pressure on their kids to perform. Whether they're living vicariously through them or can't accept anything but perfection from one of their offspring, demanding results can have an adverse affect on young athletes. They may end up hating the sport. Extreme pressure from

Mia and I will go at each other when the Philadelphia Charge takes on the Washington Freedom in the WUSA. But after the game, we're simply two friends who have shared a lot of great experiences.

parents can also spill over into other aspects of their relationship and be hurtful. That's really sad when that happens. Keep the enjoyment of the sport in your perspective.

I get motivation by creating it now—a quote from someone about me or my team, a dirty look, or anything I can use. When I first started playing, however, other elements stoked my internal flame. I'd hear murmurs from coaches and parents that I was too small to be a threat. I'd hear, "She's so tiny. She's so little." That would drive me nuts and completely fire me up. Even if I'd score three goals in a game, they wouldn't credit my play, but rather discredit my opponents. They'd say, "How can you let that little runt dominate?"

Comments like that can still get under my skin a little bit today. So consider this a warning, don't let me hear you say something like that. I'll take you down!

Find your own source of motivation and run with it. It helps build pride in yourself and gives you a sense of direction. You'll be surprised at what you can accomplish by following what motivates you.

Using Failure to Motivate

No athlete, no matter how good, has ever coasted through his or her career without being confronted by personal failure. It's a part of sports. The greatest basketball player of all time—fellow Carolina alumnus Michael Jordan—suffered a failure before attaining greatness. During his sophomore year at Laney High School in North Carolina, Jordan was cut from the varsity team. Despite believing that he should have made the squad, Jordan decided to make the most of a temporary setback. He averaged twenty-five points a game for the junior

UNC–C for Competition

As of 2002, the University of North Carolina women's soccer program has won sixteen of the twenty-one NCAA national championships since the inaugural women's title game in 1981. Several factors have led to that high degree of dominance, but the main reason is that the program is based on competition.

Everything you do in practice at Carolina is recorded. And I mean everything! Your times in sprints, the number of headballs won, the accuracy of your shots, and the outcomes of one-on-one battles with teammates are all recorded. Every day, the team manager, Tom Sanders, enters the statistics into a computer program which automatically ranks each player in every category. The categories and rankings are posted weekly. So depending on how many players are on the team, say there's twenty-two, players are ranked one through twenty-two in each category.

This accomplishes three things. First, it has a psychological impact on you. It forces you to concentrate on everything you do at practice because your execution is constantly scrutinized and recorded—every shot, every pass, every sprint, every scrimmage. So there is no time for slacking because it will show up on paper.

Second, it creates a very competitive atmosphere because all of your teammates become your competitors. Most of the players at Carolina are high school all-Americans or highly accomplished athletes, so a lot of personal pride is instilled in each individual. No one wants to see her name at the bottom of a list.

Last, it documents in black and white what your personal strengths and weaknesses on the field are among the best college players in the country. If you're ranked second on the team in shooting, but nineteenth in heading, then you're cognizant of an area in your game that needs additional work. Take pride and improve your strengths, but focus on weaknesses in practice to become a more complete player.

So everything we did at practice was about building a strong, competitive mentality. I think that's why there are a lot of Carolina athletes on national teams. It's not just because of the winning tradition and attracting great talent, but because playing in the program psychologically hardens you so you are prepared for the next level if that's what you aspire to.

varsity team, gave up playing baseball the following summer to work on his game, and made varsity the following season. He averaged twenty points per game as a junior and began to attract the attention of college recruiters.

The rest is history—literally.

Failing at something is only negative if you don't learn from it. Why did you fail? Did you do everything you possibly could have to succeed? If you did, then I wouldn't consider it a failure, possibly a bit of bad luck, which is beyond the grasp of your control. But more often than not, you could have done something more to maximize your effort. Sometimes it's difficult to be objective when it comes to evaluating yourself, but deep down, you probably know the answer to your struggles.

I went through an experience like this in 1996. After earning a roster spot on the national team, I was selected as an alternate on the Olympic team. I was only seventeen years old at the time, so I wouldn't consider this a major setback, but I was really disappointed. I thought I was supposed to be on that team. But eventually, I looked back on it and realized that I didn't deserve to be on the roster.

During the 1996 season (leading up to the Olympics), I played in a lot of games with the national team and earned a bunch of caps (game appearances). But I only played the last ten or fifteen minutes of games. I thought coming off the bench and participating in practices would be enough to maintain my conditioning. I didn't realize that you had to condition on your own to stay fit. When it came time to select the Olympic team, I simply wasn't fit enough to compete at that level.

Reflecting back on that experience, I was fortunate to learn an early lesson at age seventeen. I think I expected to make that Olympic roster and didn't work as hard as I should have. From that moment on, I swore to myself that they would never keep me off the national team because of fitness. Being named an alternate became a source of motivation. Today, I can go all out on the soccer field for the entire ninety minutes. I owe that motivation to 1996.

Sacrifice

I can't even begin to count the hours of practices, games, and tournaments that I compiled growing up playing soccer. But never once did I consider any of it a sacrifice. Playing soccer is what I loved to do, so I never felt as if I were missing out on something better. My best friends played soccer, so they were right there with me most of the time. I'm still having the time of my life playing soccer, so if some people consider it a sacrifice, then spell mine with a capital S.

When you're young, it's easy to take playing soccer for granted. It's always been there for you to play. You may not realize how much you love the game until the opportunity to play is gone

from your grasp. I've been injured a few times and unable to play, and that's taught me how important the game is to me. I despise the feeling of not being able to play, and it affects other aspects of my life.

You have to make choices along the way, and sometimes you're forced to surrender an event or gathering you'd like to attend. Say, for example, there is a surprise sweet-sixteen party for one of your good friends, but you're going to be out of the state that weekend playing in a holiday tournament. Obviously, you'd like to go to the party, but think about all the great experiences you'll have at that tournament. You get to see other parts of the country, hang out with your teammates in hotel rooms, eat at different restaurants, and maybe even shop a little. It's like your own little party when your team goes away. Oh yeah, and you get to play a bunch of soccer games against new competition as well and have a chance to win a tournament.

Whenever I had to pass up on something in my personal life, I tried to keep my focus on the big picture. I'd weigh out the positives and negatives of each and the scale would always tip toward soccer.

I only wish that I had more time for the people I love. I don't get to see my family and close friends from home as much as I'd like to. At this point, I'm pulled in all sorts of directions with the sport. It's not so much the sport itself; it's everything that surrounds it—the travel, the ever-changing schedule, the not knowing if an appearance is going to be forty-five minutes or four hours. But all of that builds character. In one respect, you've got to be very disciplined and structured when playing a sport as a professional. But another aspect requires you to be very flexible and to be able to respond quickly and positively when something changes last minute. I'm pretty laid back, so I'm okay with that. If I weren't, I'd have probably driven myself nuts by now.

My best friend in the world, Jennifer "Pooh" Medina

A FAIR ASSESSMENT

Jennifer "Pooh" Medina
Best friend and former teammate

"The first time I met Lorrie was when she was ten years old. She and Ronnie were trying out for the Sunnyvale Roadrunners. The two of them were little speed demons all over the field. I can remember when practice was over, they were waiting for their father to pick them up and they were so excited. It was Friday night and I couldn't believe how eager they were for him to get there. I found out that Friday night was pizza night in the Fair family and, thus, was introduced to the joyous obsession over food in the Fair household."

Playing Aggressive Soccer

To succeed on the field, you've got to play aggressively. It's not something that can be taught. Rather it's a decision that you have to make. It's entirely mental. It's about courage, determination, and an absolute willingness to do whatever it takes to win the ball. Don't play timidly, because if you're hesitant going into a play, you're beat.

It takes courage to go into those tackles full force. But you learn very quickly that if you don't go into a play with everything you've got, ironically you become more susceptible to injury. The player who goes in less than 100 percent is the one who is more likely to get hurt.

People often commented on how aggressively I played at a young age. My answer to that was simple—I just wanted the ball. I'd do anything necessary to come away with the ball at my feet. My brother once had the nerve to say to me, "You know, Lorrie, you're fouling a lot of players out there." This is coming from the guy who had been body slamming my sister and me ever since we could walk! I replied, "Well, I wonder how I developed such an aggressive nature?"

I think it's terrible for a coach to tell a player that she's being too aggressive. I once had a coach tell me to tone down my aggression, that I might hurt someone by tackling so hard. That really affected my play. When you're younger, and your coach tells you that you're doing something wrong, you believe him or her and start doubting yourself. Being aggressive was part of my style of play. I wasn't the same player without that tenacious approach. It took me a long time to get that edge back.

My advice is to play as hard as you can, all the while staying within the rules of the

There is nothing wrong with playing aggressive soccer. In fact, I think it's the only way to play.

as "the zone." When you're in the zone, you perform flawlessly. Most athletes can get into the zone for a short period of time, but the goal is to make that time extend as long as possible to try to sustain it.

Positive thoughts breed positive results and visualization is a method of engaging positive thought. I guess I would describe visualization as using your imagination with a purpose. You visualize something positive and attempt to build off of that mindset.

There are two different paths to travel when using visualization. You can refer to or recall a positive experience from the past. It may be a goal you scored, a tackle, a perfect pass, or winning a headball. You call up that imagery from your memory and try to feed from it, using all of your senses so that the image is as real as possible. The second path is to imagine something positive happening in the future. Picture yourself faking out an opponent, making a great trap, hitting a perfect cross, or, my favorite, celebrating a game-winning goal.

When to use visualization is up to the individual. Some of my teammates practice visualizing the night before a game, others ten minutes before competition, and some use it during the game. Find out what works best for you.

game. Don't become apprehensive because your opponent's approach is to play with trepidation. If two players go into a tackle aggressively, the chances of injury decrease and play continues.

Visualization

The mental aspect of the game is very important during competition. It's about trying to train your mind so you get into what people refer to

Eliminating Doubt

Athletes are pretty strong-minded, but we're also human. When something goes wrong, you tend to start doubting yourself. When you doubt yourself, your confidence suffers which causes you to make more mistakes. Suddenly, you find yourself struggling to execute simple tasks. To stop that downward spiral, find something to refer to that allows you to say, "Okay, I'm playing poorly. It's time to turn things around." One of my teammates has a little wristband she pulls at, or other girls will bend down and grab their shin guards. Maybe you can retie your shoes or snap your hair tie to symbolize that you're ready to stop the bleeding and pick up your play.

I really haven't figured out my "little thing" yet. I've talked about it with the sport psychologist for the national team. One thing I focus on is self-talk. I always make sure that I use positive words. I'll say to myself, "This is my headball," or "Stick this girl hard." I never use negative self-talk because it promotes doubt. Never say things like, "Don't screw up," or "Don't lose the ball." If you think bad things, bad things will follow.

The University of North Carolina

I mentioned previously that in explaining my rise through the ranks, I give some credit to good fortune. I'm not too proud to admit that a little luck never hurts your pursuit toward accomplishing goals. In most cases, you make your own luck, but there have been instances where my timing couldn't have been better. My introduction to University of North Carolina head coach Anson Dorrance was one of those instances.

During the summer after my junior year in high school, I was playing in a North versus South state-tournament game in California. Anson was at the game, but I didn't know he was there or even who he was. I was playing center forward, and during that game, scored the goal of my life. I stripped the ball from a defender, did a one-two around her, and drilled a shot into the upper 90 of the goal. I think I was as shocked as everyone else.

Not only was I fortunate that Anson was there to see a great goal, but the capper was that Anson prides himself on teaching his offensive players to defend. He gave a lecture to coaches and players later that night, and actually used my goal as a reference in his speech. You can imagine how I felt. He contacted me about playing at Carolina the next week.

The Competitive Side of Lorrie Fair

"If you really want to agitate Lorrie, just beat her at something—anything."

—Greg Fair (brother)

"Lorrie has a competitive nature about her that you cannot instill. It's part of her persona."

—Anson Dorrance (UNC women's soccer head coach)

"The girl is competitive with everything. Everything! I know this might sound crazy, but she used to play hide-and-go-seek . . . by herself! She'd play against her stuffed animals. Now you tell me how you're supposed to lose in that game?"

—Pooh (best friend)

"One of Lorrie's best attributes is her tenacity. Once she makes up her mind to do something, she'll put everything she's got into making it happen."

—May Fair (mother)

"The competitiveness between the two of us was absolutely crazy growing up. I couldn't even begin to list the things we battled over. It was everything. There were times when we literally raced home from school to see who could get to the bathroom first. Can you imagine going all out and the grand prize is a toilet?"

—Ronnie Fair (twin sister)

Selecting a College

Much like every high school junior and senior, selecting a college was a difficult ordeal. I was being recruited for soccer and decided to draw up a list of five schools that would satisfy two aspirations. First, I wanted to attend an institution that would be academically challenging.

A moment with my Carolina teammates and coaches after defeating the University of Notre Dame 2–0 to win the 1999 NCAA women's soccer national championship. It was the third national title during my tenure at UNC and the only way to go out my senior season.

My mother has always stressed the importance of education, and I agreed with her 100 percent. My grades and boards in high school were very good, so there was no reason to set my sights any lower than a university with a reputation for outstanding academics. Second, I wanted to continue playing soccer in college. So I focused on schools with exceptional academic standings that were equipped with strong soccer programs.

I went on five recruiting visits. I went to Notre Dame, the University of Portland, Stanford, Duke, and North Carolina. I visited Carolina last, and after that, I had no second choice. Once I went down and I stayed on the campus, met several professors, and spoke again with Anson, it was a no-brainer. My mom was hoping I'd stay on the west coast and go to Stanford (which is where Ronnie went), but in my heart, it was Carolina Blue all the way.

It was funny that the weekend of my recruiting visit was when they hosted the women's soccer national championship in 1995. Carolina ended up losing the national semifinal game at home to Notre Dame, ending a string of nine consecutive national titles. You could say I was a little uncomfortable having to stay with team members that night. The last thing they wanted to do was take care of a recruit after they had just lost for only the third time in history. I can remember Tiffany ("Tiff") Roberts and Beth Sheppard arguing back and forth, "You take her!" "No you take her!!" Despite the loss, they ended up showing me a great time.

Playing for Anson Dorrance in the Midst of a Dynasty

The University of North Carolina women's soccer program was founded in 1979. Because the NCAA did not yet offer women's soccer, Carolina played in the AIWA (Association of

Having my number retired at the University of North Carolina was one of the proudest individual achievements of my life.

Fair is Fair

At Carolina, Anson Dorrance always used to say that if you're someone who people label as having potential, well, it means you're not worth all that much right now. I'm not a big fan of the term *potential*. I mean, try to define it. How do you really know what your potential is? You don't. Even if you get to the highest possible level of play, is that your potential? Maybe it is, but maybe it's higher than that. You may be among the best, but perhaps your potential is to be the best of the best. And if you do become the best of the best, is that your potential? Should you stop trying to enhance your game?

The bottom line is you should never be satisfied with where you are or be content with what you may become. You can always—always—improve some element of your game, and there is no time like the present to begin working on it. Talking about potential is fantasy. In reality, and this is true in all facets of life, people are interested in what can you do today—right now.

Intercollegiate Athletics for Women). The Tar Heels played a regular-season schedule in 1979 and 1980 before the AIWA sanctioned a national championship tournament in 1981. UNC won its first national title in 1981, capping off a perfect 23–0 season. In 1982 the NCAA offered a women's soccer national championship, and Carolina claimed the first-ever NCAA national title.

Since its inception in 1979, the UNC women's soccer program's winning percentage is an astounding 94 percent! That means for every 100 games we play, our average record is 94–6. If you don't believe me, call the UNC athletic department and ask them to send you a copy of the women's soccer media guide.

Success breeds success, and Carolina attracts some of the most talented players in the country each year. But I think the way Anson runs the program is the number-one reason why Carolina has been so good for so long.

Anson treats his players like young adults. He grants players a lot of freedom and trust. Anson understands that college is an environment where you find out which direction you want your life to take. You discover your interests and what you're passionate about. Whether it's math, science, art, student government, clubs, soccer, or your sorority, there is an abundance of opportunity on campus to do different things and meet different people. Anson encourages players to get involved in a variety of activities.

We didn't really have any rules on our team. Anson felt that rules displayed a lack of trust. The program he has built and the caliber of players on each roster enables him to do that.

Making the National Team

With my national team teammates at the 2000 summer Olympics in Sydney, Australia. Participating in the Olympics was just one of the many unbelievable things I've experienced through playing the sport I love.

In 1995, I was invited to the U.S. Olympic Festival. It was just after the U.S. women's national team lost in the 1995 World Cup semifinal game to Sweden. The staff was giving the national team time off and brought in a group of new players to observe in training camp. After camp concluded, the coaches called me in and told me that I'd played very well.

A month later, I received a phone call and was invited to the next camp, in September, followed by another in October, and a final camp in December. The coaching staff was looking to finalize the new national team roster that would train for the 1996 Olympics. Training began January 1st, and if your name was on the roster, for six months you lived and trained in Orlando, Florida, with the team. I checked the list and my name was on it and I can't even describe to you how fired up I was when I saw that.

Versatility

One reason I was selected was because of my versatility. I could play many positions on the field, and the staff considered that to be a valuable asset. (All positions except for goalie of course. You don't see too many 5' 3" goaltenders on national teams.) There were only sixteen spots on the Olympic team roster. There are only eleven on the field, and you need one back-up goaltender. That left four players on the bench to cover every position on the field. Those players had to perform wherever they're needed.

I could play offense or defense because I played so much soccer in my life. When I was a

The fact that we had all-Americans on our bench waiting for a chance to play allowed Anson to extend that freedom to us.

At the same time, players learn quickly that they have a strict responsibility to the team. You can do whatever it is you want with your free time, but if the manner in which you spend that free time adversely affects the team, then there is a problem. You can test the waters, but more often than not, it's going to come back to bite you. Our goal each preseason is to win the national championship. With sixteen out of twenty-one possible national championship trophies in our possession, nothing less is acceptable at UNC.

Our practices were one-and-a-half to two-hours long. After practice, you were free to do whatever you wanted. But that ninety-minute session was all about soccer. Every thought, every physical act, and every conversation revolved around soccer. It was very intense, but after it's over, you return to being a normal college student.

kid playing center forward, I learned to play defense because I was running all over the place trying to get the ball. If the ball wasn't at my feet, I was like a crazed lunatic and would race around to strip the ball from the dribbler.

It paid for me to be versatile, and you should never shy away from trying a new position at your coach's request. First, he or she may see something in you that shows you're better suited for a different position. Second, learning to play another position is an opportunity to expand your skills and increase your value as a player.

I hope I've helped you to understand that developing into a solid soccer player entails more than speed, strength, and foot skills. Your body will only take you as far as your mind allows. The forthcoming chapters will discuss the basic fundamentals of the game in detail; but to become the best you can be, your qualities must include the intangibles such as passion, competitiveness, and mental toughness.

A FAIR ASSESSMENT

Julie Foudy

U.S. women's national team captain

"Lorrie has been a valuable player on the national team because she's multidimensional. She can play so many different positions on the team. We talk to young kids all the time about the benefits of learning to play different positions. It's a great asset to possess. Lorrie can play defense and midfield, and she also has offensive skills. I think she's best suited for the midfield because she can showcase all of her talents."

"When you put a uniform on,

you're representing something

that's bigger than you."

Rules and Equipment

Soccer is a pretty free-spirited game. I mean, where else can you run around a field that is a hundred and twenty yards long by eighty yards wide for ninety minutes? Play never stops unless there's a foul or injury, and poor weather rarely postpones games. It just makes them more interesting. And with the exception of the specific rules that apply to the goalkeeper, any player on either team can perform any act (within the rules) on any part of the field. That's pretty cool, especially when considering other outdoor sports.

In softball, hitters have to wait for the pitcher to throw the ball and are permitted to run only between the baselines. Tennis players are restricted to one side of the net and only have possession of the ball for service every other game. And I have no idea how field hockey players maintain their sanity. They're only allowed to use one side of the stick and seemingly every time they take a step, a whistle is blown for obstruction. I respect these athletes who can abide by such restrictions.

Although there is vast freedom in soccer, the game is based around a set of rules that provides a basic structure to keep games fair and competitive. To perform within that structure, it's important to learn the rules of the game, understand its etiquette, and to respect the sport, officials, and opponents. You can have the greatest natural talent in the world, but unless you play within soccer's guidelines, those skills will be devoid of any potential use.

Sportsmanship Versus Gamesmanship

Each of these terms, *sportsmanship* and *gamesmanship*, is critical to your development as a player. They're so important that I've dusted off my dictionary to offer you a concise definition of each term.

Sportsmanship is conduct becoming to a sportsman—a person who is fair and generous, a humble loser and a graceful winner. Graciously shaking your opponent's hand after a loss, giving credit to the insurmountable efforts of

It's Fair to say . . .

I can remember one game at UNC where one of my teammates nearly made a monumental error that would have had us running sprints until dawn the next morning. We were playing a game and had a 9–0 lead. We all knew it was time to stop scoring. Meredith Florance came off the bench and into the game. She was a freshman and excited to get out on the field. Well, all of sudden, she's got the ball at her feet with nothing but an open field and a goalkeeper in front of her. So she takes off with the ball to goal. We're all screaming, "No!!" It wasn't that she was defying Anson, it was just that she got caught up in the game, and her instinct took over. She went in for the one on one and blasted a shot just inches left of the goal.

I can tell you this; our players were much more relieved that she missed the shot than any member of the opposition. If she had scored, we might still be running today.

the opposing team after a defeat, or showing respect to a team you've soundly beaten are all signs of sportsmanship. It's conducting yourself in a manner that illustrates pride in yourself, your team, and the organization or institution you're representing. Sportsmanship is not something that is innate; it is learned, accepted, and exercised by understanding the difference between right and wrong. A person who displays sportsmanship emanates strong moral fiber. It's a sign of maturity.

Most people relate the term *sportsmanship* to losing. You've all heard the phrase, "She's a poor sport." I can tell you that I learned a lot about sportsmanship at North Carolina, even though we rarely lost. Anson taught us about sportsmanship through different channels. He wanted us to be competitive and approach each game with relentless energy. But there is a dif-

ference between defeating a team and humiliating them. Once we had a safe lead and it was clear the opposing team had no legitimate chance of beating us, we'd stop shooting on goal. We'd continue to work on other parts of our game, but why run up the score? It makes you look bad, and inevitably, it will come back to haunt you.

Gamesmanship is the art or practice of winning games by questionable expedients without actually violating the rules of the game. Sounds kind of shady doesn't it? You get the image of a bunch of lawyers running around in soccer shorts. Well, it's not shady. It's a matter of observing subtleties during the game and using them to your advantage. For example, during the initial stages of the game, you may notice that the referee is allowing players to tackle aggressively. While one official might interpret the tackle as a foul (or violation of the rules), another might view it as a strong, but clean tackle. If this is the case, tackle with more ferocity. This is called gamesmanship. It is feeling out the elements of each game from the referee, to the weather, to the opposing team, and using them to your advantage by integrating them into your winning strategy.

Another example is that a linesman may be missing offsides calls continuously. If you're an attacker, take advantage and get a little behind the defensive line if you're not going to get called. It may give you a competitive edge, and ultimately, a scoring opportunity.

Both sportsmanship and gamesmanship are elements that augment your worth on the soccer field. Make each a member of your arsenal.

Equipment

To get yourself on the field of play, you've got to wear the proper equipment. Soccer players are notorious for trying to stretch rules to the limit when it comes to what they wear. Part of

When we put on our uniform in the WUSA, it's all business. However, we still manage to have our fair share of fun.

that is due to comfort, but I'll admit it, some of it is driven by fashion sense.

But seriously, your uniform and equipment worn is not simply about the way you look. Protective gear—such as shin guards—can help prevent injury and give you a greater sense of security. Wear what the guidelines specify so you can focus on what's important—the game.

Putting on the Uniform

In everyday life, you're representing yourself. You set out to do the best you can in whatever you're doing because it's a reflection of your character. When you put on a uniform— whether it's a school uniform, work uniform, or athletic uniform—you're representing something that's bigger than you are. In this case, it's the team.

A Fairly Embarrassing Moment

When I was sixteen or seventeen years old, my best friend, Pooh, and I would referee youth league soccer games to make some money. Usually, we would ref a game in the morning and then play in a game or tournament in the afternoon. Pooh and I would wear our Sunnyvale Roadrunner warm-ups to ref the game. We thought they were a lot more fashionable than the referee's uniforms.

One morning, the game we were officiating went into overtime, and we were running late. I called Ronnie and told her to bring our uniforms straight to the field so we could change under our warm-ups. I think all girls become masters at changing their clothes under their sweats. So we get to the field and our team was warming up. Pooh and I quickly changed on the sideline.

Before the game started, the ref had everyone meet at midfield to check our jerseys, shin guards, and player cards. So he comes over to me and says, "Lorrie Fair, number seven." At this point, I should have had my warm-ups off so my number was displayed, but because it was cold that day, I still had my sweats on. So I pulled down my sweat pants to show the ref my number on my shorts. The problem was that because I was so rushed, I kind of forgot to put my shorts on underneath.

So there I stood, flashing my Daffy Duck underwear to the referee. (They were a gag gift, but quickly became my lucky pair.) I soon realized that the cool breeze was a little brisker than usual, and I pulled my pants up as fast as I could. The ref told me, "Why don't you try putting your shorts on and then come back." So I turn around, and a swarm of people in the stands behind me were laughing hysterically.

I haven't watched a Looney Tunes episode the same way since.

When I played AYSO soccer, I represented the Blue Streaks, the Maroon Marauders, and the Killer Karrots. (We came up with our own nicknames for teams in AYSO because we had a lottery for team colors. Who wouldn't get fired up playing for a team called the Killer Karrots?) They may have just been youth league soccer teams, but when I was a kid, they were part of my identity. Once I advanced to club soccer, I represented the 1978 Sunnyvale Roadrunners. But that team was made up of players from all over northern California, so personally, I was also representing my hometown of Los Altos.

When we won the State Cup in 1994, our team represented the state of California in the regional tournament. Once we won regionals and advanced to the national final championship, we represented the western region of the United States.

Regardless of what your uniform jersey reads, you have a responsibility to your family, teammates, organization, and, ultimately, yourself to perform your very best. Every time I put a uniform on, I take pride in giving everything I have on the field. I like to think of myself as a laid-back person who is easy to get along with, but once I put on the jersey, I leave that personality behind and get busy.

Soccer Shoes

The name of the game is comfort when it comes to footwear on a soccer field. You've got to wear shoes that feel comfortable on your feet but also keep your mind at ease. You need to feel secure that you're wearing the right type of shoes for the surface you're playing on. There are enough areas of concern to deal with during the game. Your choice of boots is not something that should be on your mind.

I like my shoes really snug on my feet. My old shoes were like a pair of slippers. They were broken into the shape of my foot, and it was like putting on a pair of socks. The soccer shoes

I wear are made of kangaroo leather. I don't like the synthetic material because it feels like there's something between the ball and my foot. The kangaroo leather gives me the feel that the ball is right on my foot.

Cleats versus turfs. The surface of the field dictates the type of soccer shoes you wear. Short grass, long grass, wet grass, firm ground, and artificial turf are all elements that can determine the type of shoes you decide to lace up. I always bring several pair of shoes to each game—screw-ins, molded cleats, and turfs. I'll go with my instinct in selecting the type of shoe and wear them during warm-ups. If I feel like I need to make a change, I'll do so before game time. During the game, it may rain or the ground may thaw, so it's nice to have different shoes in my bag to make an adjustment at halftime if necessary.

I like to wear screw-ins whenever possible because I feel like they give me the best traction. My style of play calls for a lot of cutting, so I need something to dig into the ground to help me change direction. Some girls don't like screw-ins because they've been injured using them. I've heard them say that they feel as if they might get stuck in the ground when they cut, or that the pressure from the cleats on the bottom of their feet is painful. I guess it's all a matter of personal preference.

The most popular type of shoe worn is one that has molded cleats. Molded cleats can be worn on nearly every surface—long grass, short grass, and so forth. I don't prefer molded cleats when the ground is a little wet or soft. Mud, grass, and dirt get caught up between the cleats and before long, you feel like you're wearing flats. This is where screw-ins or longer studs come in handy.

When playing on artificial turf or really hard surfaces, wear turf shoes, which have a large number of really short cleats on the bottom of the shoe. My home field for the Philadelphia Charge is artificial turf. We play at Villanova

When playing on natural grass, cleats are usually the best form of soccer shoes to wear.

Wearing shin guards is part of the package when playing competitive soccer. They may protect you from suffering a serious injury.

Stadium (800 Lancaster Avenue, Villanova, Pennsylvania—tell them Lorrie sent you.) so I'm pretty familiar with wearing turf shoes. Personally, I'd much rather play on real grass, but that's a whole other book.

If the surface is really hard, I'll wear turfs as well. Cleats are unable to dig into the ground and you can slip or lose your footing. If you're unsure, try each shoe during pregame and decide which feels more comfortable.

Tips for kids. When you're purchasing a pair of soccer shoes, leave about a half-an-inch cushion between your toes and the end of your shoe. Your feet are still growing and if you buy a pair that fit perfectly, you'll grow out of them quickly. This not only gets expensive, but the life of the shoes never lasts long enough to break them into the mold of your foot.

Take care of your cleats by keeping them clean and treating them with leather food. The shoes will last longer and Mom and Dad will be a whole lot happier.

Socks and Shin Guards
I like to wear only my game socks with no excess material between my foot and my shoe.

However, if the game socks are really thin, I'll wear a pair of ankle socks over my game socks. Pull the game socks up over your shin guards. I know, you hate to wear them, but you have to. They protect you from getting kicked and suffering a potential injury.

At Carolina, we used to practice without shin guards for the purpose of learning when to jump. When you have no chance of getting to a ball first, it's best to jump. It avoids an unnecessary risk of injury. I'm the last person who would ever tell you not to play aggressively, but there are times when it pays to be smart and protect yourself. Go in hard on every tackle, but if you have no shot at the ball, take to the air. It will save you a nasty bruise.

Shorts
I wear a pair of sliders under my shorts when I'm playing on artificial turf. That's the only time, though, because sliders can restrict my hamstrings and risk a strain or pull. Playing for the Charge on artificial turf, sliders are an absolute necessity. Your legs will get completely torn up on turf without wearing them. Wear your team shorts over your sliders. Always try to get a pair that fits.

A FAIR ASSESSMENT

Greg Fair
Brother

"Dinner at our house growing up was ridiculous. We would fight over food. I was recently thinking about it and I think every family argument that we had originated at the dinner table.

"We had one dinner table rule where you had to finish everything on your plate and everything in your glass. Usually, that was not a problem. In fact, if you turned your head away from your plate long enough, someone would swipe food right off your plate.

"Well, one time I got up from the table to get another glass of milk. Another dinner rule was that if you got up to fill your drink, you had to refill anyone else's glass upon request. So of course Lorrie had finished her milk but waited for me to get up to get a refill. So I grabbed a thirty-two-ounce cup from the kitchen and filled it to the rim. You have to finish everything in your glass, right?

"I put the cup down and we noticed there was milk coming out of the bottom. It had a leak. So we started yelling at Lorrie, "Hurry up! Drink it! Drink it!" Lorrie slammed a thirty-two-ounce cup of milk. Talk about mind over matter. Ronnie and I were in hysterics. I think Lorrie was bloated for about six hours.

"And I'm pretty sure she got her own refills for quite a while after that."

Shirt

I like wearing long sleeve shirts underneath my uniform jersey, even if it's just a little cold. Being from California, I don't ever like to be cold, so I like long sleeve shirts. During the game, though, you sweat a lot and can catch cold if you're wearing short sleeves. I try to pack at least one extra shirt when playing a game in case I need one that is dry.

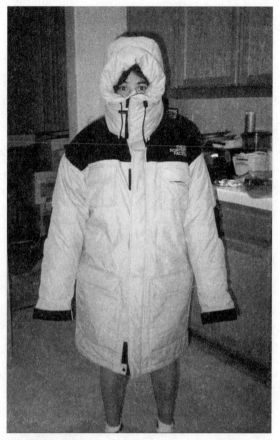

It's pretty safe to say that my sister Ronnie can be classified as a warm-weather person.

Artificial Turf

Because I brought up the subject of artificial turf, I might as well talk about it. You probably get the idea that I don't like it. Well, I don't. Even its title bothers me. How could anyone like anything that is predicated by the word *artificial*? Would you ever want to order an artificial cheeseburger? Would you care for an artificial day at the spa? How about having an artificial boyfriend? Or would that be superficial? Anyway, the point is that artificial turf changes the game. It takes something that is pure and taints it a little bit.

The biggest thing about playing on artificial turf is that the ball moves a lot faster. You've probably noticed this playing indoor soccer, but it's a much larger factor outdoors on a

Artificial surfaces (or turf) play differently than natural grass. The ball bounces higher, skips quicker, and rolls much faster. These are just a few factors that force you to adjust your game.

bigger field. Your touch has to be better, you have to pass more to feet, balls skip if it's wet, and they bounce high. Turf is an arena for players who are technical. The better ball-handling skills you possess, the more successful you'll be on artificial surface.

Because the surface is quicker, you need to factor in a few things when playing on turf. When sending a lead pass to a teammate, you have to adjust your pass in one of two ways. Either slow down the pace of your pass, or lead your teammate less.

Every artificial turf is unique, so use your time in warm-ups wisely. See how the ball reacts when bending or putting spin on the ball. Take shots on goal and watch to see if the ball skips and takes off on the goalkeeper. If the surface is a little wet, I'll hit shots that short-hop the goalie because they're much more difficult to handle. The ball may skip past her or rebound off her for a scoring chance.

Rules

The rules of soccer have generally stayed the same since the game's inception. Some rules have been tweaked a bit, like the offsides rule. It used to be that if the offensive player was even with the defender, she was offsides. Now, if you're even with the defender you're still on.

One of the more recent changes deals with the goalkeeper. The goalie can now take as many steps as she likes with the ball, but has to release the ball within six seconds. I love this rule change. It stimulates the transition game and creates an immediate offensive threat. The goalie can run up to the eighteen-yard line and send the ball into the attacking third of the field almost instantaneously. If defensive players make runs out of the backfield, they may not be able to get back before the ball from the goalkeeper is delivered.

If I could change one rule, it would be the overtime rule. I don't mind the golden goal (first team who scores a goal wins), but I'm not a big fan of shootouts. I realize that our 1999 World Cup championship title was decided by a shootout, but I still think it's a horrible way to lose a game. Penalty kicks should never decide a game's outcome, especially a game of that magnitude. A shootout doesn't necessarily favor the better team.

At one time it was suggested that a game was to be decided by the number of corner kicks. The team that compiled the most corner kicks during the game would be declared the winner. But I don't think a game should ever be determined by a statistic. Who decides which stat is the most important?

Referees

Refereeing a soccer game is a pretty thankless job. Rarely do you hear a comment like, "The U.S. women played really well, but did you notice the incredible performance by the refs?"

The rule change regarding unlimited steps for goalkeepers creates opportunity for a quick offensive transition out of the backfield.

Comments made about the referees usually include a few choice words, followed by blame. Honestly, one of the best compliments you can give refs is to not even notice that they were there. That means they kept control of the game with little interference.

How to Talk to Refs

Inevitably, referees will make bad calls or showcase inconsistency in their calls. When this happens, should you go ballistic and tell the ref he or she stinks? No, you should not. But that doesn't mean you should say nothing at all. There is a right way and a wrong way to make a comment to a ref. The difference is in tone and tact.

Let's say an offensive player is tripped from behind while making a pass, but the ball is going onto a forward's foot who has a great scoring chance. The ref whistles a foul. Here is the right way to handle it: calmly say, "Ref why would you call that?" If he or she answers that a foul had been committed, I would then say, "Did you see where the ball was? I would rather have the ball on our forward's foot running to goal uncontested than have ten opposing players line up behind the ball as I receive a free kick."

And that's it. The ref is not going to change the call in that situation. The play is already dead. But you do want to let them know that they made a poor decision in whistling the foul. First, you hope he or she won't make the same mistake twice, and second, the ref may give you a payback call later.

How Not to Talk to Refs

The wrong way to handle the situation is to use dissent. That is what will get you a card. "That was a terrible call! You stink! You shouldn't even be refereeing! Get your vision checked!" That will get you nowhere, except possibly being issued a yellow card.

And don't use sarcasm either. Refs don't like sarcasm. It's a form of dissent.

Testing the Waters

Players test the waters for the first fifteen to twenty minutes of every game. It's usually pretty frantic. You're testing the other team, attempting to weather the emotional storm that unravels in the early goings. But you're also trying to test the referee.

The first tackle you make, you always want to stick really hard. If you get called for a foul, that's okay. You want to set a high standard for a foul. If the ref does not call it, then you know you can get away with playing extremely physical. Factor that into your play for the rest of the game, because you can bet your opponent will. Remember that's called *gamesmanship*.

While soccer referees may vary in their interpretation of certain rules, it's important to understand that for that game, their judgment is the law.

Beginner's Guide to the Basic Rules of the Game

Because the game of soccer has experienced such rapid growth in recent years, many newcomers to the sport have never watched or played the game. For those of you who are looking for a basic introduction to soccer, please read the information that follows to familiarize yourself with the general rules of the game.

Soccer is a game played by two teams of eleven players. The object is to put the ball in the opponent's goal. The team that scores the greater number of goals wins the game.

The **duration** of the game depends on the level of play. International and collegiate competitions are played in two forty-five-minute halves. High school contests are two forty-minute sessions. Youth league games are shorter and are often split into quarters.

The **playing field** is rectangular and must be 50 to 100 yards wide and 100 to 130 yards long. At each end of the field is a goal area. The goal—centered along the goal line—is 24 feet

Fair is Fair

You know what I would do if I could set the overtime rules? First I'd get rid of the penalty kicks altogether. I like the golden-goal format: the first goal wins. I'd have the two teams play two full fifteen-minute overtime periods of golden goal. If no goals are scored, I would then go to five-minute overtime periods, but at the beginning of each one, a player from each team is pulled off the field. How cool would that be?

By reducing the number of players, the game's outcome would become a test of stamina, resolve, and mental toughness. Who wants it the most? I just hope if that ever happens, and it gets all the way down to one versus one, that we're playing the New York Power and Ronnie and I are squaring off against each other. Winner gets the second plate of food at the dinner table. Now that would be a battle.

long by 8 feet high. A crossbar adjoins two goalposts. A mesh net outlines the inside of the goal.

Each **team** has eleven players on the field. The goalkeeper is the only player on the team permitted to touch and handle the ball with her hands and this is only allowed within the penalty area.

The **penalty area** is indicated on each end of the field of play by two lines drawn at right angles to the goal line, 22 yards from the midpoint of the goal line. These lines extend into the field of play for a distance of 18 yards. The ends of these lines are joined by a line parallel to the goal line. The lines are part of the penalty area.

The **ball** is to be spherical, with a circumference of at least 27 inches, but no more than 28 inches. The weight of the ball has to be at least 14 ounces, but no more than 16 ounces. The outer casing of the ball should be leather or

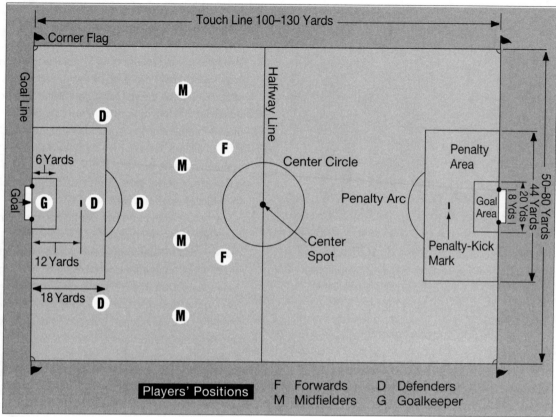

FIGURE 2.1
A regulation soccer field

other material that is similar and weather resistant. It's the responsibility of the home team to provide three or more game balls.

A **referee** officiates the game. Depending on the level of play, a game might have a single referee, two referees, or a referee who is assisted by two linesmen. The referee maintains control of the game, acts as the timekeeper, keeps a record of the game, and enforces the rules of the game. Referees are responsible for starting and restarting the game, stopping the game because of an injury, declaring whether or not the field is playable, deciding whether play should continue or be postponed in the event of poor weather conditions, and cautioning or sending off players who harshly violate the rules or etiquette of the game. The referee also

has the authority to dismiss coaches or spectators who are unruly and interfere with play on the field.

The **linesmen** indicate when the ball is out of play and which side is given possession to put the ball back into play with a throw-in, corner kick, or goal kick. They also call offsides during a game.

A **substitute** is a team member who is not on the playing field. The substitution rule varies depending on which organization's rule you're playing under. In high school soccer, the number of substitutes allowed in a game is unlimited. Under FIFA rules, a maximum of two substitutes is permitted per game. Once a player is substituted for, they may not reenter the game.

To **start play**, the ball is kicked while it's stationary on the ground at the center of the field. At the moment of the kickoff, all players are to be on their team's half of the field. The ball must move forward and may be played by any player on the field except the one who kicked off. The referee initiates play by the sound of the whistle at the start of each period and after goals.

Fouls or Violations

Except on throw-ins, the goalkeeper is the only player permitted to play the ball with her hands (within the penalty area). A player, however, may use any other part of the body—feet, head, chest, and thighs—to play the ball.

A **direct kick** is awarded to a team if the opponent commits one of several fouls or violations. A player may score a goal off of a direct kick. The kick is placed at the spot of the foul. The ball may be kicked in any direction, and each opponent must be positioned no closer than ten yards from the point of the kick. Any player of the offended team may take a free kick.

Direct kicks are awarded when:

- A player spits, kicks, or strikes another player

- A player trips, attempts to trip, holds, pushes, or charges at another player

- A player deliberately handles, carries, strikes, or propels the ball with a hand or arm

- A player charges into the goalkeeper

- A goalkeeper attempts to strike or push an opponent with the ball

An **indirect kick** is awarded to a team if the opponent commits one of several fouls or violations. A player may not score off of an indirect kick. The ball must be touched or played by at least one other player on the field. An indirect

It's Fair to say . . .

There are situations where player intimidation can influence the way a referee is calling the game. Mia is the perfect example of that. If Mia is not getting calls, she'll let the ref know, and usually they'll listen. Mia gets banged around and tripped a lot, so if she's not getting calls, it's going to be a long day for her.

Carla Overbeck is another one who uses intimidation, but hers is the more literal sense of the word. Some of the things she says to refs crack me up. But because Carla has been around so long and she's such a great leader on the field, she gets away with more than most players would.

kick can be awarded inside the penalty box if the violation falls under those that warrant an indirect kick.

Indirect kicks are awarded when:

- A player is called offsides

- A player charges into another player when neither is within playing distance of the ball

- A player obstructs an opponent who is attempting to play the ball

- A player attempts to kick at the ball when it is in the possession of the goalkeeper

- A play is considered a dangerous play (e.g., high kicking, playing the ball on the ground)

- A goalkeeper takes more than six seconds to release the ball

- A game is stopped because of misconduct by a player, coach, or spectator

That's me taking a corner kick for UNC.

the lines of the corner, nearest to where the ball left the field of play. An offensive player may not be called offside on a corner kick, but may be called offside on a subsequent play.

A **penalty kick** is awarded when a foul, which ordinarily results in a direct kick, occurs within the offending team's penalty area. The ball is kicked by an offensive player from the twelve-yard line. All players, except the kicker and goal-keeper, remain on the field of play but outside the penalty area. The goalkeeper must stand on the goal line between the goalposts until the ball is kicked. Lateral movement is allowed, but the goalkeeper may not come off the line by step-ping or lunging forward until the ball is kicked.

The ball may not be played again by the kicker until another player touches it. If the ball hits the post, the shooter may not play the rebound. If the ball deflects off the goalkeeper, however, the shooter may play the rebound.

A **throw-in** is awarded to a team when a ball last touched by the opposing team travels over the end line. The ball may be thrown in any direction from the point where it crossed the end line. The thrower must use both hands with equal force and deliver the ball from behind and over her head in one continuous motion. Both feet must remain on the ground behind the end line.

A **goal** is worth one point and is scored when the entire ball legally passes beyond the goal line. It must pass between the goalposts and under the crossbar provided it has not been deliberately thrown, carried, or propelled by the hand or arm of an offensive player.

- A player is injured and the ball is clearly in one team's possession

- A kicker taking the restart plays the ball before another player touches it (e.g., corner kick, free kick, goal kick)

A **goal kick** is called when a ball last touched by the attacking team travels out of bounds over the goal line. The defensive team is awarded a direct kick and may place the ball anywhere within the goal area. Opposing players must stand outside the penalty area and may not play the ball until it has cleared the penalty area.

A **corner kick** is called when a ball last touched by the defensive team travels out of bounds over the goal line. A corner kick is awarded to the offensive team. The ball is kicked within the quarter circle, including on

Make sure you take the ball straight back over your head with two hands when executing a throw-in. Being called for a foul throw is an inexcusable way to lose possession.

A goal may be scored from:

- A kickoff
- A direct kick
- A goal kick
- A penalty kick
- A corner kick
- A drop ball
- A goalkeeper's punt, drop-kick, or throw

A goal may not be scored directly from:

- An indirect kick
- A throw-in
- A free kick into a team's own goal

That summarizes the basic rules of the game. For greater detail, purchase an official rulebook from your league's association. But with a basic understanding of soccer's guidelines, we're now ready to move forward and discuss the fundamental skills of the game. So lace up those cleats and let's take the field.

"Young players need to handle

the ball as much as possible."

Dribbling

All right, I'll be perfectly honest. When I was growing up, I was a ball hog. In fact, when I played in the American Youth Soccer Organization (AYSO), a lot of my teammates probably wanted to tie me to a chair. I always wanted the ball, and if I didn't have it, I'd go get it. I was so bad that at times, I would take the ball away from my own teammates. Ronnie would do it too. (Sorry, Sis, but if I'm going down, I'm taking you down with me.) My coaches constantly yelled at me. "Lorrie! Stay in your own position!"

I know that a girl hogging the ball can be a sensitive subject, especially among parents. But looking back, I think it was a major factor in my development as a player. Constantly having the ball at my feet allowed me to feel comfortable with it at an early age. Because I took on player after player, I learned to dribble under pressure, dribble out of pressure, dribble for speed, and dribble creatively. I watched professional soccer players—men and others who were better than me. I would try to emulate their moves.

I refined my moves through trial and error in the game and became familiar with what type

My first love and long-term relationship: me and the soccer ball

It's a Dirty Job, but Somebody . . .

I remember, during one of my first AYSO games, a huge mud puddle was in the middle of the field. It had to be eight feet long and six feet wide. Inevitably, the ball landed in the middle of the puddle. Play just stopped. Everyone was just standing around the mud puddle looking at the ball. I wanted to go get it, but I was afraid I'd get so muddy that my mom would kill me.

My dad was standing on the sidelines, and I heard him yell out, "Come on, Lorrie, go get it!" Well, that was all I needed to hear. I sprinted into the puddle and kicked the ball out. Of course, my standing leg slipped from underneath me and I landed flat on my back. I was covered in mud.

My dad literally had to hose me off before I got home. If I showed up at home and my mom had seen me as filthy as I was, I would have been the youngest homeless girl in Northern California.

Dribbling at your opponent forces her to commit to defending you.

of moves worked in certain situations. Dribbling in practice helps, but nothing conditions and improves your skills better than game execution.

Now, I'm not trying to coax everyone into becoming fanatical dribblers. My point is that young players need to handle the ball as much as possible. When you're growing, the ball can feel awkward at your feet. Establishing comfort with the ball at an early age sparks the development process for other areas of your game.

Dribbling requires the ball to be at your feet, and the more the ball is at your feet, the more opportunities you have to improve other skills such as passing, receiving, and shooting. You'll also enhance your field awareness. No longer will you have to look down at the ball because you'll always have a sense of where it is. With your eyes up, you can look for open teammates,

see how the defense has shifted, or know where the goalkeeper is positioned.

When to Dribble

As I'll discuss in Chapter 4, "Passing," the ball moves much faster than the players. The quickest way to move the ball is to pass it. That said, at times, dribbling is a very effective method of moving the ball and creating opportunities. Always remember that when the ball is at your feet, you possess what everyone else wants. The opposition is forced to pay attention to you, and you can use that possession—that bargaining power—to your advantage. And if they don't want to pay attention to you, keep the ball at your feet and make them pay.

Dribbling is something you can use anywhere on the field. Use it to chew up space, get out of tight spaces, create space for yourself, create space for a pass or shot, or to challenge a defender one on one. Dribbling is a basic element of soccer.

Allow me to give an example of a good time to dribble the ball. Let's say you have the ball and you're in a two-on-one situation. The defender is shuffling backward trying to figure out whom to pick up—you or the overlapping runner. If you immediately pass the ball to the overlapping runner, the defender is simply going to shift over to defend your teammate. But, if you hold onto the ball and dribble at the defender, it forces her to make a decision. She can go with the runner or take the ball. More often than not, she's going to commit to defending you (because you have the ball). Once she commits to you, flip the ball to your teammate. You've now created a situation where your teammate is running onto the ball full speed, and the lone defender has no chance of recovering.

The best reasons to dribble are:

- To force the defender to commit to you or your teammate

- To escape from tight spaces under defensive pressure

- To create space for a pass or shot

- To take on the defender—a one-on-one situation

- To chew up space if the forwards and defenders are running away from you

- To slow play down and get numbers to your advantage

When to Get Rid of It

When I first joined my club team, I played forward. I was able to outrun people and because of that, employed a raw style of dribbling that relied on speed. The way I dribbled wasn't

Dribbling can be used to take the offensive or avoid danger. Here, I'm taking the ball back away from the attacker to maintain possession and find an open teammate.

perceived as a weakness because I was still scoring goals. Eventually, I was moved back to the sweeper position because it was a gap that our team needed to fill. When I started dribbling the ball out of the back, I'd hear moans from my coach, Frank Medina (Pooh's dad), on the sideline. "Lorrie," he'd say. "I'm turning gray over here."

If you're faced up dribbling out of the backfield, do not take on the attacker. It's too dangerous. In the offensive third of the field it's okay, but in the midfield or defensive third, you're the last line of defense. Attackers will apply intense pressure on you in hopes of forcing a turnover. They know that if they can strip you, they're taking it in for a one on one with the goalkeeper.

Dribbling can also slow down play during an offensive attack or transition if you're not dribbling up to the speed of play. If you have numbers up (more numbers attacking than the opposition has defending), dribbling at a speed less than the speed of play allows defensive players to recover and mark up. Keep play moving and pass the ball to teammates or open space.

Last, offensive players often fall so in love with beating defenders that they forget their main intent, which is to put the ball in the back of the net. Don't sacrifice results for artistry. If you have an open shot or a teammate is in a dangerous position to score, hit it. The scoreboard does not keep track of how many players you've challenged and beat. It records the amount of goals scored.

It is often best to get rid of the ball when:

- Receiving pressure from an attacker in the backfield

- Dribbling out of the backfield with an attacker approaching to apply pressure

- During an offensive attack or transition (don't slow down play)

- Becoming too cute with the ball; too many touches

Too Close for Comfort

For any of you daredevils who play in the defensive backfield, listen closely to this story. You might think twice before making a flashy move after reading this.

When I played for my club team, the Sunnyvale Roadrunners, we advanced to the under-16 national championship. We had won the state cup tournament, and then won the regional tournament before moving on to the title game.

In the final, we were leading 1–0 with thirty seconds remaining. I was playing sweeperback, and the opponent sent a ball high over my head. I ran in the direction of my goal to get the ball. Meredith Florance, an attacker for the Dallas Sting who later became my teammate at North Carolina, was chasing behind me. The ball was bouncing, so I tried to flick it up over my and Meredith's heads, so I could quickly spin around her and run onto the ball on the other side of her. Only I didn't flick it high enough.

The ball cleared my head, but Meredith jumped up and took the ball off her chest. While I turned to run upfield, Meredith's momentum was going to goal . . . with the ball. She had a one on one with the keeper. She ripped a shot, and it missed wide to the left by only a few inches. We held on to win the game 1–0 and claimed the U-16 national championship.

Fortunately for me, I learned a valuable lesson, minus the catastrophic results. Trying to be innovative or creative on the soccer field is great, but there is a time and place for everything. That was not the right situation to try that move.

I don't know how I would've lived with myself if she had scored. In my mind, I can still see that shot today. The funny thing was that following the game, I had to rush to get on a plane to fly to Germany with the U-19 national team. If Meredith had scored, the game would have gone into overtime, and I would have missed my flight to Germany.

The Fundamentals of Dribbling

Dribbling is the most basic skill in soccer. The goal is to advance the ball while running, all the while maintaining control of it. Essentially, you're pushing the ball down the field using light taps with the inside, outside, or instep of your foot. Your touches should be soft enough so that the ball is never more than a step away from you, which enables you to keep your head up.

With open space in front of you, increase the distance of your touches. Push the ball forward so that you touch it every two steps. This allows you to run faster with the ball. Do not, however, touch the ball too far in front of you. The

Use the top portion of the outside of your foot to dribble straight.

ball must be close enough at all times to make an immediate pass or fire a shot.

I wasn't a tight dribbler when I was younger. I was fast and relied on quickness to beat defenders. Once I started playing club soccer, other players would be just as fast as I was. If I touched the ball too far forward, I'd lose possession. I don't think it's an understatement to say it would drive me completely NUTS when I lost possession of the ball! Consequently, I began to employ tighter touches to maintain control of the ball . . . and my sanity.

Straight Dribbling

To dribble the ball straight, use the top portion of the outside of your foot. Point your toe down as you tap the upper half of the ball. The top of your foot represents the longest extension of your leg. Using it to dribble allows you to keep the ball at the perfect distance. It's far

enough away to immediately strike a pass or shot, but close enough to touch it to avoid an encroaching defender. Use the inside of your foot as if you're cutting or changing direction.

Good dribblers are able to touch the ball in stride as they're running. This is possible only if you're able to dribble the ball with both feet. You *must* become proficient at dribbling with either your right or left foot. While you're running (especially when dribbling fast), you cannot predict which leg will come up in stride when it's time to touch the ball. If you're uncomfortable dribbling with one foot and have to stutter-step to use the other, you'll slow down and give the defense a chance to recover. At varying speeds, practice using both feet.

If I were training a kid to dribble, I'd have her touch the ball every other step—left touch, step, left touch, step, and then switch feet. I'd have her start very slow, and over time, increase her speed. As the player progressed, I'd then have her touch the ball every step—left, right, left, right. Eventually, she will develop touch and the ability to dribble with both feet.

Dribbling with your head up allows you to see the field.

Balance requires strong muscles in your legs, hips, lower back, and abdominal regions.

Keep Your Head Up

The purpose of dribbling is to get into a position to shoot, create space for a pass, or relieve pressure. With your head down and eyes on the ball, you can't possibly see what opportunities are available. Keep your head up as you dribble to see the field.

You might miss the following if your eyes are glued to the ball:

- The opportunity to shoot on goal. You may be closer to goal than you think.

- A wide-open teammate. Great passes require great timing. The window of opportunity only lasts so long.

- An incoming defender. Opponents can and will come from all different directions to strip the ball. Don't simply rely on the shrieks of your teammates.

- A goalkeeper out of position. You may be twenty-five yards out and the goalie has wandered out near the six- or eight-yard line. A simple chip can land softly in the back of the net. You have to see her positioning to cash in on her mistake.

Keep your eyes up and reap the benefits.

Balance

Never underestimate the importance of balance. Balance affects every aspect of your game, not just dribbling but shooting, passing, heading, and changing direction. Without balance, you'll struggle with your game. As you dribble, stay on the balls of your feet with your weight leaned slightly forward. This enables you to

To dribble to the left, use the inside of your right foot or outside of your left (as shown here).

MY PERSONAL HAT TRICK

Top Three Favorite . . .

TV shows	"Friends," "Will & Grace," "Cosby Show"
Movies	Animated *Robin Hood, Friday, The Thomas Crown Affair*
Books	*The Power of One, The Notebook, The Great Gatsby*
Magazines	*InStyle, Sports Illustrated, GQ*
Musical Performers . . .	Janet Jackson, Madonna, my brother (Greg)
Songs	Otis Redding, "Sittin' on the Dock of the Bay"; Maxwell, "This Woman's Work"; Tupac, "California Love"
Places to Shop	King of Prussia Mall, New York City, Wal-Mart
Foods	Steak, cheese, guacamole
Hobbies	Crosswords, people-watching, beach volleyball
Personalities	Meg Ryan, Michael Jordan, my twin sister
Classes	Public speaking, physics, math

move forward, stop, cut, pass, shoot, or shield the ball.

At times, you will have to take on a defender while dribbling. The objective is to get the defender off-balance so that you can explode past her with the ball. If *you're* off-balance, it's impossible to be explosive. Suddenly, the prey becomes the hunter, and you become the hunted.

Dribbling Left to Right and Right to Left

To dribble to the left, use the inside of your right foot or the outside of your left. Lean to the left and push off of the leg that is not touching the ball. To dribble to the right, use the inside of your left foot or the outside of your right. Shift your body to move in that direction.

You can also use the sole of your foot to move the ball left and right. The Brazilians are exceptional at using the soles of their feet, and it's very difficult to defend them one on one. There is no real indication to which direction they'll take the ball, so you have to be careful. With the sole of the foot, the ball can be moved in any direction . . . forward, backward, and to the side. Try it yourself and you'll see.

Dribbling Moves

Our forwards on the national team are all one-on-one artists. Their strengths lie in taking on and beating defenders with the dribble. Most of our outside midfielders are one-on-one artists as well. They're often isolated on the outside with their mark and play a one-on-one battle throughout the entire game. We try to get the ball to the forward's feet so she's faced up as much as possible. She's quick and can beat defenders into the space behind, but if we can get her the ball so she's faced up one on one, we'll take that any day.

To beat defenders, you've got to have some dribbling moves available in your bag of tricks. Some moves are very simple while others are more elaborate. Some of the moves that I use now are the same ones I used when I was twelve years old.

Always remember that it's not the quantity of dribbling moves that's important, it's the quality of them. You're the salesperson and have to convince the defender to buy. If your sales pitch is no good, no sale. Develop a few moves that you're comfortable using in the game and work on perfecting them.

Certain players have a knack for selling certain moves extremely well. Physical size and speed can factor into determining which moves suit you. Cindy Parlow, for example, uses the scissors move all the time (the scissors move is discussed later in this chapter). She's got long legs and she's pigeon-toed, making it easy for her to sweep over the ball with the outside of her foot. My legs are a little shorter and I might trip if I try to do too much stuff over the ball. Most of my footwork is done behind or with the ball.

Accelerating to Speed

Great dribblers aren't necessarily fast, but they're explosive. Mia, Tiffeny "Millie" Milbrett, and Cindy are examples of attackers whose first two steps are extraordinarily explosive. If they get the defender flat-footed or leaning one way for just an instant, they're gone. And to get a shot on goal, all you need is a little bit of space.

To be explosive, you've got to be traveling at less than full speed. If you're going full tilt at a defender, you can't accelerate to any speed. When you're making a move, slow down before executing it. This is standard for nearly every dribbling move. Dribble hard at the defender so they're backpedaling a bit. Slow down just before you make your move, so that they slow down with you. Now throw your move—whether it is a feint or a step-over—and then accelerate.

Those first two steps are what make Mia and Millie so good. They get a brief window of opportunity and blow past the defender. To get the most out of those initial steps, get low and explode with everything. Explode with your legs, your hips, and your arms and shoulders. Your entire body needs to burst into the direction you're dribbling.

An element that separates great dribblers from the rest of the pack is their ability to accelerate to speed quickly.

The purpose of a feint is to get the defender to "bite" to one side and then explode past her in the opposite direction.

It's difficult to be explosive if you're standing straight up. Most likely, your first movement will be to crouch down and then go. Think about sprinters taking off for a race. Their starting position is on the ground, which allows them to burst upward and accelerate to full speed as quickly as possible. It's no different with a soccer ball at your feet. Stay low to generate maximum power and quickness.

Feints

Many dribbling moves rely exclusively on body movements. The ball remains untouched while you attempt to deceive the defender with jukes and fakes. Feints are often used to initiate a move but, if they're convincing enough, can be used independently to dupe the defender.

A feint is an upper-body fake combined with a jab step. It's used to coax the defender into moving her feet and shifting her body to defend a direction that you're not going. By getting her to lean to one side, you can beat her to the opposite side. It's just like in football. How do you think running backs fake out defensive players. They dip their shoulders or body, step to one side, and then explode to the other.

Suppose you're dribbling down the left side of the field and want to make a move to the right to go to the goal. Slow down to get the defender to slow down. Take a deliberate step to the left as if you're about to explode past the defender. Your eyes, upper body, and hips should all face to the left to sell the feint. Shift your weight onto your left leg and lean forward with your upper body. The ball remains stationary.

After your left foot plants, square your upper body to the left and shift your weight forward. Begin to take a step with your right foot in that direction. In midstride, however, push off to the right with your left foot. Explode to the right

A cut to the inside (across your body) is more of a "chopping" movement made with the inside of your foot.

past the defender, taking the ball with the outside of your right foot.

Feints can also be used to give you the extra space to deliver a pass or take a shot. Regardless of their purpose, feints must be convincing to be effective. Rushing through them or doing them half-heartedly will render them useless. Sell the feint and you're in business.

Cuts

Cutting with the ball means that you're dribbling hard in one direction and then you quickly change your direction. This is one move that doesn't require you to slow down. It's most effective when you're dribbling at a fast pace.

There are two basic types of cuts: to the inside of the defender and to the outside of the defender. Typically, defenders play you toward the outside of the field. Dribbling down the right sideline, the defender will angle her body toward the sideline to force you that way. A cut to the inside would be to your left and toward

the middle of the field. A cut to the outside would be to your right and toward the sideline.

A cut to the inside is a sharper cut. It's a chopping movement that requires a more severe change of direction. Let's say you're making a move from right to left. Take the ball with the inside of your right foot. The direction of your cut should be on a diagonal line to the left. If the cut is too sharp (or lateral), the defender will have time to adjust her feet and stay in front of you. If the cut is not sharp enough (too vertical), it may be too close to the defender allowing her to get her foot on the ball.

As you make the cut, shift your entire body to the left immediately. Quickly realign your shoulders, hips, and feet to face to the left. The defender is now forced to adjust her feet, giving you a brief opportunity to explode past her into space and cut her off. Your first two steps are extremely critical. If you can get past the defender before she shifts her feet and stays in front of you, you're by her. The only way for her to stop you is to foul you.

The key to cutting to the outside is to fake to one side, stop your momentum with your plant leg (in this photo it's my left leg), and then take the ball with the outside of your right foot.

The step-over move: For this demonstration, I'm standing to the right of the ball (top left). Step over the ball with your right foot (top right), drag your left foot behind you and plant. Shift your momentum to the right and take the ball with the outside of your right foot (above).

Obviously, the ability to get your body to swiftly change direction is essential when cutting. But those first two steps *after* the cut are equally important. The cut inside is a simple move, but dribblers who master them demand respect from the defense.

The cut to the outside is similar, but usually requires a fake to the inside before cutting to the outside. Defenders are more conscious of defending the goal side and will quickly react to movements toward the middle of the field. A fake inside can coax them into adjusting their feet (and balance), giving you a window of opportunity to explode to the outside.

The ball is then taken with the outside of your foot. It's not as sharp a cut as the inside cut. It's more of a vertical path than a lateral one. Your change of direction is not as drastic on outside cuts, so you should be able to bolt past the defender with just a little bit of room. Once you are past her, cut back inside to cut her off.

Step-Over

Step-over moves are fairly simple to employ and can be used in various forms. Step-over moves take some time, so use them when you have open space and are attacking a defender. Tight spaces are not always conducive to step-overs.

With the ball on the left side of your body, step over the ball with your right foot. Your left foot will sort of drag behind as your right foot lands on the opposite side of the ball. Plant on your left leg and push the ball to the right with the outside of your right foot.

This move is sold by making the defender believe you're taking the ball in the direction of the step-over side. Make sure your head, shoulders, and hips square up as you feint to that side. The defender will shift or lean to that side, leaving her susceptible to the opposite side. Quickly plant and change direction.

The step-on turn: Approach the ball as if you're about to kick it long and step on the ball with your kicking foot (top left). Take a little hop in front of the ball with your left foot, so you land on the opposite side of the ball (top right). Plant and shift your momentum, taking the ball to the left with the outside of your left foot (above).

Variations. You can use several variations to the step-over. I often step behind the ball. As long as my feint is believable, I'll get the defender off-balance. Feints are often what fake the defender out because they often stare at your upper body.

You can also use a double step-over, which means you step over the ball twice. This works

in one of two ways. Either the defender doesn't bite on the first step-over and falls for the second, or she falls for both and screws herself into the ground.

Step-On Turn

The step-on turn is best used when you have the option of a long pass or shot but would rather keep the ball and change direction. Perhaps your teammates are yelling to send a cross-field pass to switch the field of play, or you have a good look at the goal from twenty-five yards out. Whatever the circumstance, your options will improve by beating the defender. The key to the step-on is to make the defender believe you're gearing up to strike the ball with authority.

With the ball at your feet, pretend that you're going to drive the ball with your instep. Look upfield to what the defender thinks is your intended target. You want her to rush forward to block the kick.

Take a full backswing and as your kicking leg thrusts forward, raise your foot and step on top of the ball. Put on the brakes and stop your weight from shifting forward. Take a little hop forward with your plant leg so it lands on the opposite side of the ball. Take the ball with the outside of your standing leg foot and go.

The scissors move: To accelerate to your left using the scissors move, start with the ball on your right side. Sweep around the front of the ball in a clockwise motion (left). As your right foot lands to the right of the ball, sweep behind the ball with your left foot, so the ball is now on your left side. Take the ball to your left with the outside of your left foot (right).

Cruyff

The Cruyff move is similar to the step-on. Use it when you might kick the ball for distance—a cross, switching fields, or a clear.

Say you're pretending to strike the ball with your right foot. Instead of stepping on the ball, chop the ball behind your left foot. Take a short hop forward with your left foot (plant leg), and then drag the ball with the inside of your right foot behind your left leg. Turn your body to the left and accelerate.

Scissors

The scissors move takes a little time and space to execute but is effective when a defender is running toward you. I had a friend who loved to use the scissors move. In fact, she'd do it when nobody was on her. She'd be dribbling down the middle of the field with no one on her, and all of a sudden, break into a scissors move. It was kind of funny.

The scissors move requires you to step in front of the ball rather than over it. With the ball on your left side, take your left foot and zip around the front of the ball. Your right foot trails behind the ball and finishes with the ball to its right. Push the ball with the outside of your right foot and explode to the right.

Stanley Matthews

One of my favorite moves is the Stanley Matthews. I like it because it's a move that combines body movement and movement of the ball.

With the ball on your right, pull it across your body to the left with the inside of your

right foot. Then, quickly push it back to the right with the outside of your right foot. The key to this move is a hop with your left foot. As you're dragging the ball across to your left, hop to the left with your left foot. That hop acts as a feint to the left. So you hop and feint to the left, and then quickly explode to the right.

Because the ball and your body are moving to the left, the defender is certain to move to her right. That provides you the opportunity to burst past her to her left. Quick feet and timing are essential to this move. I practiced it a lot growing up and use it all the time in games.

Shielding

Shielding allows you to maintain possession of the ball. You shield the ball from the defender with your body. The key is to put distance between the defender and the ball.

Another function of shielding is that it allows the ball handler to kill time. When strikers check back to the midfield to receive a pass (running away from the goal they're attacking), they often have to hold the ball and wait for teammates to make runs forward. Shielding the ball allows you to maintain possession as your passing options get forward.

You can use your body to shield the ball in two ways. The first and best method is to position

Stanley Matthews: This is one of my favorite moves. It requires quick feet. Pull the ball across with the inside of your right foot (top) and take a quick hop forward with your left foot. Immediately push the ball back to the right with the outside of your right foot (above). This move happens very fast and is useful in tight spaces.

your body sideways to the defender. This places the most distance between the defender and the ball. Lean into the defender and contact her with your forearm. Use your forearm to hold her off

When shielding the ball, lean into the defender with your arm or upper body. Keep the ball on the outside of your foot (top) or control it with the sole of your foot (above).

It's Fair to say . . .

When you have no one in front of you and defenders are chasing, by all means give the ball a good whack and sprint after it. Understand that the players chasing you are running without the ball, so if you try to dribble the ball ahead into space, they'll catch up quickly.

After you make your move and get past the defender, your next explosive touch should be to cut off the defender so that she can't run along side of you. Force her to chase you from the back so she can't stick her foot in to poke the ball or slide tackle you.

You can even hit the ball into space with a defender facing you. I've seen Tiffeny Milbrett do this a ton of times. When Millie has the ball and there are twenty yards or more space behind the defender, she'll bang past her and sprint onto it. The key is to run to the opposite side that the defender turns. If you run into the side she turns, she'll obstruct your path to the ball. (Of course if you're strong like Millie, you can kindly shoulder the defender out of the way.) Millie runs to the backside of the defender, knowing she won't be able to keep up with her. That's not called *kick-and-run soccer*. It's called using your strength to your advantage.

because she's going to be pushing you. If the defender is able to get underneath you, lean into her with your shoulder to fend off her pressure.

Keep the ball under the sole of your foot. You'll be able to move the ball in any direction by using the sole. Hold your arms out for balance. This is essential because with the ball under your foot, you're standing on one leg.

The other method of shielding the ball is to back directly into the defender. Get as low to the ground as possible and stick you rear end out to increase the distance between her and the ball. Keep your arms out for balance and also to feel which side the player is attacking. If she attempts to bolt around your left for the ball, quickly take the ball to your right.

Playing with "Sole": The Brazilians

The Brazilians are the best in the world at using the soles of their feet to manipulate the ball. As I mentioned earlier, they're tough to defend because they can move the ball in any direction at any time. They can pull the ball right or left, forward or back, and there's no movement leading up to it that hints to which way they're going.

I adjust my approach on defense when we play Brazil. I play them really tight off the ball but am very careful not to stab or jump at the ball once a player receives it. I play tighter on them to slow them down so someone can come over to double team. If I'm right up on a player when she receives the ball, she can only move in the direction she's facing, which most likely is with her back to the goal.

If I give her too much space, it allows her to face up and run at me. When that happens, she's able to move the ball in all different directions and it's very tough to defend.

Chances are that you're not going to strip the ball from a Brazilian by yourself. It's only going to happen if someone comes over to double team. I try to deny them from turning, which slows play down, and ultimately gives one of my teammates time to attack her.

I play aggressively on them without the ball and stay patient once they get it.

Here I am pictured with members of my extended family: Cindy Parlow, Mia Hamm, and Carla Overbeck.

This drill trains the dribbler in three important skill areas. First, it forces her to keep her head up as she dribbles. With all the traffic, the dribbler must be looking up to avoid hitting another player. Second, it teaches the player to keep the ball close to her feet as she dribbles. And third, it develops the ability to dribble in tight spaces.

After the coach blows the whistle, stop and rest. Hopefully the ball will be at your feet and you managed to avoid any fender benders inside the circle.

Soccer Slalom

Place twelve cones in a straight line, positioning them approximately two feet apart. Starting from the first cone, weave in and out using just the insides of your feet. Have a teammate use a stopwatch to measure the time it takes you to get through the last cone.

Next, use just your right foot to dribble through the cones. Start by using the inside of your feet, then touch with the outside, inside, outside, inside, outside, and so forth. Keep control of the ball, and check your time when you finish. On your next trip through, use only your left foot (inside, outside, and so forth).

Drills

Mass Traffic

Have the entire team stand in the midfield circle. Each player has a ball at her feet. On the coach's whistle, begin dribbling at game speed staying inside the circle at all times. Practice your feints, cutting, and swift changes of direction.

Try to improve your times each session. To give the drill a little more spice, gather some teammates and see who can score the best time. There's nothing like a little competition to accelerate your improvement.

Creative Dribbling

Stand eight cones in a tight space in random places. Dribble through the cones as quickly as possible while using feints and various game moves. Try to pass through each cone without dribbling through the same way twice. This improves your agility and also enhances your comfort level with your dribbling moves.

Be creative and challenge yourself to diversify your dribbling skills. Remember to practice at game speed, because it's the only way to develop confidence in your dribbling moves.

It's Fair to say . . .

When you're dribbling the ball, a simple glance upfield or to the side can give you room to operate. Even if I just take a look, the defender has to shift a little in anticipation of a pass. That quick glance might put her off-balance and enable you to dribble past her.

"A good passer makes her

teammates look good."

Passing

I had a coach named George Lamptey who used to refer to passing by saying, "Make your teammates look good." He meant that a good passer always finds the right teammate at the right time and executes the pass so efficiently that the receiver doesn't even have to break stride. The pace is the right pace, the texture on the ball is perfect, and the pass is accurate and is put to a spot that's to her teammate's strength, not her weakness. Great passing not only makes your teammates look good, but it makes your whole team look good.

The Importance of Passing

Soccer can often be a game of circumstance and situation, but one fact remains indisputable. *The ball moves faster than the players.* I don't care if Marion Jones is playing for one team, and Gail Deevers is playing for the other. A passed ball is going to get from point A to point B faster than any player who dribbles with the ball. My club team was called Roadrunners, and even with a nickname like that, the ball could outrun us. To move the ball quickly, whether you're advancing it forward or moving it laterally, you've got to pass it.

The ball simply moves faster when it's passed rather than dribbled. Here, I've delivered a lead pass to my Philadelphia Charge teammate Jenny Benson.

Beginner's Tip

When making a pass with the side of the foot, the ankle locks so the foot is set at a ninety-degree angle. When I'm instructing at youth camps, one of the most difficult elements of passing to teach young kids is getting them to lock their ankle without locking their entire leg. I tell them to relax their leg so it swings back and forth and preach that the power comes from their hips. I have them continuously swing their leg back and forth and then tell them to, "Pull your toe up to your kneecap." This forms the ninety-degree angle they need to strike a push pass. Remember, the power comes from your hips and your leg remains relaxed.

Although dribbling is essential in soccer, it can slow down the flow of play when you're on an offensive attack or transition. The element of surprise is limited when attacking at a moderate pace. Defenders can set up tight on their mark to deny the ball, recover on a mark who may have broken free, or even double up on the dribbler. The defense is able to anticipate better and minimize the offense's options.

Once the ball is passed, however, the situation changes. Defenders must now adjust their positioning and redetermine which players or areas on the field now present the greatest danger. A second pass followed by another quick pass, and now the defense is constantly readjusting. Passing is about unpredictability and creates scoring opportunities.

Mixing It Up

In international competition, teams such as Norway, China, and Germany are very familiar with our style of play. To beat defenders, we sometimes have to vary our passing attack just to keep them honest. Let's say we're passing everything to the feet of our attackers. Well, what is the defense going to start doing? They're going to push up tight to our forwards and kick them at their heels because they know the ball is coming on the ground to our feet. To counter, we'll then spray a ball over the top of them and try to let our attackers run onto the ball. The attacker may beat the defender and win the ball or she may not, but the defense will be forced to back off a bit, which allows us the space to once again pass the ball on the ground to feet. It's like a game of cat and mouse. When we vary our services, the defenders can't as easily anticipate where the ball is going.

In its most basic form, the object of the game is to get the ball past eleven players and into their goal. One person dribbling is not going to cruise through eleven players (even though I used to love trying to do it as a kid). To win, soccer requires you to work together as a team. Passing is a method of getting everyone involved and creating scoring opportunities.

The Passing Fundamentals

Passing is an important skill that needs to be taught to young players. I try to keep things simple in the beginning and teach kicking with the inside of the foot first. From there, you can learn various methods of passing the ball, such as passing with the outside of the foot, instep passes, chipping, and bending the ball. The mechanics for each type of pass are very similar in form and technique, but each has its own style and purpose.

A great way to practice passing is hitting the ball against a wall. Walls are great, especially if you're by yourself. My garage door suffered quite a few hits (as did the garage windows) courtesy of Ronnie and me. You can practice everything: push passes, instep drives, outside of the foot, bending balls, even volleying. To work on your accuracy, put some tape up like goalposts and aim for the corners with the inside, outside, and instep of your foot.

The Push Pass

The push pass is primarily used for short passes on the ground (up to approximately twenty yards). It is the most basic and accurate form of passing the soccer ball. An overlap pass, a wall (or give and go) pass, a backward pass, a short-lead pass, and a close-range shot are examples of when a push pass can be used. Because there is very little backswing when delivering a push pass, it takes minimal time to execute and is very efficient.

Technique. When executing a push pass, use the inside of your kicking foot. Stride forward and place the nonkicking foot beside the ball a little less than the ball's width away. Position the plant foot so it points to the target. Your plant

leg is slightly flexed at the knee to help keep balance. Hold your arms out away from you to also maintain balance.

Turn your kicking foot outward and lock your ankle so it's positioned at a ninety-degree angle. The toes of your kicking foot are elevated slightly higher than your heel. The foot remains square to the target throughout the kicking motion.

Whenever possible, square your hips and shoulders to the target. This optimizes the accuracy of your passes. Often, you'll be on the move or have to make a last-second adjustment and are unable to square up. This is okay. As long as your hips are square to your target at contact, your passes will arrive on the mark.

As your kicking foot swings backward, lift it slightly above the ground. The length of your backswing depends on the size and strength of your legs and distance of the pass (ranges from approximately two to twelve inches). When hitting a push pass, however, you generally use a short backswing. As you take your forward swing, hold your arms out for balance and keep your head down, eyes locked on the ball. Strike

A push pass: A short backswing (left) allows you to make a quick, accurate pass. Use the side of your foot to strike the middle of the ball. Keep your head down and follow through (right).

It's Fair to say . . .

Striking the ball with the instep is one of the hardest things to teach. For me, hitting the ball perfect with the instep produces a sound and a feel that is difficult to describe.

A lot of kids are afraid to kick the ball with their instep because they're still growing and their feet keep getting bigger. They sometimes kick the ground and hurt themselves, causing them to shy away from using their instep.

I'd try to control the circumstances when teaching or reteaching the instep pass. Do something the girl is comfortable and familiar with, like a game of kickball. Slowly roll the ball and have her kick it for distance. Everyone played kickball growing up and knows that to hit the ball for distance, you can't use the side of your foot or your toe. She'll naturally being using her instep to kick the ball for power.

To become familiar with the feeling of the instep, sit on the ground with your plant leg bent and your kicking leg in the air. Your arms are out for balance and your toe is pointed, creating a straight line from your knee to your toes. Have someone drop the ball from above on your foot. As you strike it, the leg movement should be generated from the hip, not the knee. The ball should pop back up to your partner's hands with no spin. That's how you know you've hit it right. Become familiar with how it feels and sounds.

Short push passes should be delivered along the ground, as they are much easier to receive by your teammate. Remember, think of cutting the blades of grass with your foot.

the middle of the ball and follow through toward the target. Your kicking foot stays square to the ball throughout the kicking motion.

George Lamptey also used to say that you want to "cut the grass with your cleats." That produces a smooth movement through the middle of the ball. If you get underneath the ball, it will pop up in the air. If you hit too high on the ball, you'll stick it into the ground and

possibly trip yourself up. (In other words, total embarrassment.) To this day, when I make a push pass, I think of cutting the blades of grass with my foot.

The Instep Pass

There are two basic reasons for hitting an instep pass. Either it's a longer pass or a pass that needs to get to your teammate quickly. Instep passes can be kicked for greater distances and travel at higher velocities.

Many instep passes are driven through the air, and the ball travels quicker because there is no friction created by the ground to slow it down. You can hit balls high, but the best-case scenario is to send them about waist-high and have it land at your teammate's foot. I'm still working on mastering that pass.

Technique. Approach the ball on a slight angle. If you're kicking with your right foot, start behind and a little left of the ball. Plant your nonkicking foot alongside the ball, and lean slightly forward with your upper body. This

The instep pass is used for passes of longer distances. To drive a ball through the air, lean back slightly and increase your backswing (left). Contact the ball with the laces of your shoe and drive through the ball (right).

keeps you over the ball and decreases the chances of lofting it too high in the air. Hold your arms out for balance and square your hips to the target. Tilt your head down and lock your eyes on the ball.

Increase your backswing when hitting an instep pass. How much you increase it depends on how far or how hard you need to deliver the pass. The more power you need, the greater the backswing. Keep your knee over the ball and strike the ball with your laces. Your ankle is locked just as it is with the push pass, but your foot should point straight down like it's a continuation of your shin. Continue driving through the ball as you make contact and follow through. Straighten the knee and extend your leg out in front of you. Always kick *through* the ball when striking an instep pass. Land on your kicking foot.

(After reading all that technical stuff, now you really need to kick something.)

I think the most important aspect of the instep pass is to focus on where you strike the ball. It's a little lower than the middle of the ball (or where you would strike a push pass.) There is a time and place to zing an instep pass on the ground, and to do that, strike the ball in the middle. But generally, instep passes are most effective when they're sent low through the air.

Hitting a long cross or switching the field of play (a cross-field pass) may require you to send a ball higher in the air. In this case, plant your foot a few inches behind the spot where you would plant for a regular instep pass. Strike the ball a little lower and lean back slightly. These simple adjustments will allow you to send an elevated instep pass over those pesky defenders.

Varying the pace and distance. The length and speed of your instep passes vary by the amount of power you put into your kick. Of course, adjusting the length of your backswing and follow-through has an impact, but you've got to develop a feel for how much effort it takes to strike a ball specific distances and speeds. This is something that is individual and needs to be measured through practice. Say you need to hit a twenty-yard instep pass and it takes about 60 percent of your maximum effort to do so. Then for a thirty-five-yard pass, you may have to turn up the throttle to about 85 percent. The harder you have to hit a ball, the closer to 100 percent effort you need to put forth.

The Eyes of a Great Passer

If you approach any great passer on the field, freeze them and say, "Close your eyes. Now, tell me what's around you?" They might shock you, because they will know exactly where everyone is on the field, and who presents a passing opportunity. They have a phenomenal sense of field awareness or vision. Great passers already have a picture in their mind of what they'll do when they get the ball. It's sort of like shooting on goal. You know exactly where the goal is, so you don't have to look up to see it while you're shooting. Hege Riise of Norway is an extraordinary passer because of her technical skill combined with her great vision.

Danielle Fotopoulos is an example of a player who is so strong that she rarely varies her backswing. She adjusts the strength of her strikes on effort alone. That's what makes her such an effective striker. The goalkeeper never knows when to set because Danielle takes such a short backswing. She has the ball at her feet, and then all of a sudden—boom—she drills a shot into the corner.

I'm not so fortunate. When I take a hard shot, everyone in the stadium knows it because I have to take a bigger backswing to generate more power. I'm still working on that.

Outside of the Foot Passes

Passing with the outside of my feet is something I've really improved on since joining the national team. I'm still working on passing with the outside of my left foot. It's getting there, but there is a lot of room for improvement. I've gotten really good at passing with the outside of my right, and it's made me a much better player. For example, I can hit a cross from the left side with the outside of my right foot. Usually, your opponent is focused on defending a cross from your left foot when you're on the left side of the field. She'll do what she can to obstruct you from getting the ball to your left foot and hitting it across. Now that I can hit it with either foot, I'm more difficult to defend in that situation. And because the spin on the ball is the same as if I hit it with my left foot, the cross still bends into my teammate's run, and provides a very dangerous ball.

The greatest thing about the outside of the foot pass is that it's unpredictable. On very short passes, there's virtually no backswing. On medium or longer passes, your opponent can't focus on defending one foot because you can use the outside of one foot, or the inside of the other. If she commits to defend the inside of the foot pass, I can pass the ball immediately with the outside of my foot without the obstruction of my defender.

I strongly suggest that you practice kicking with the outside of your feet. Get to a point

Short passes with the outside of your foot are very difficult to anticipate.

A FAIR ASSESSMENT

Julie Foudy

U.S. women's national team captain

"I think Lorrie's biggest strengths are her incredible work rate and her technical ability. She's very clean on the ball. Her play-making ability is also outstanding because she has great vision and solid decision-making skills."

right foot. Then, quickly push it back to the right with the outside of your right foot. The key to this move is a hop with your left foot. As you're dragging the ball across to your left, hop to the left with your left foot. That hop acts as a feint to the left. So you hop and feint to the left, and then quickly explode to the right.

Because the ball and your body are moving to the left, the defender is certain to move to her right. That provides you the opportunity to burst past her to her left. Quick feet and timing are essential to this move. I practiced it a lot growing up and use it all the time in games.

Shielding

Shielding allows you to maintain possession of the ball. You shield the ball from the defender with your body. The key is to put distance between the defender and the ball.

Another function of shielding is that it allows the ball handler to kill time. When strikers check back to the midfield to receive a pass (running away from the goal they're attacking), they often have to hold the ball and wait for teammates to make runs forward. Shielding the ball allows you to maintain possession as your passing options get forward.

You can use your body to shield the ball in two ways. The first and best method is to position

Stanley Matthews: This is one of my favorite moves. It requires quick feet. Pull the ball across with the inside of your right foot (top) and take a quick hop forward with your left foot. Immediately push the ball back to the right with the outside of your right foot (above). This move happens very fast and is useful in tight spaces.

your body sideways to the defender. This places the most distance between the defender and the ball. Lean into the defender and contact her with your forearm. Use your forearm to hold her off

shoulders as best you can, and take a short, quick backswing. Strike the middle of the ball. (Depending on the type of shot required, adjust where you hit the ball. Do you need to elevate your shot? Hit lower on the ball. Do you want to keep it on the ground? Hit higher on the ball.)

Shots from outside the box need to be driven with the instep. In this game against Notre Dame, I drilled a direct kick right at an unfortunate group of opponents.

The Power Shot

Most players love the power shot. It even sounds cool—*power shot*. There is certainly a place for power shooting in soccer. The technique has produced many highlight film goals, but try not to fall in love with it. In most cases, there is a better option.

I can remember taking a penalty kick at UNC in a game against Colorado. I can't really remember the score, but I do recall the outcome of my actions.

After the ref blew the whistle, I hit a shot that the goalie blocked. The ball came rolling right back out to me, and as you know, once another player touches the ball, the shooter can play it. Well, I was so mad that the keeper saved my shot. I glared down at the ball rolling out to me, and all I had in my mind was blasting a shot into the goal. I wasn't going to be satisfied just beating the goalie; I wanted to put a hole in the net. So from about eight yards out and facing a fallen goalie, I cranked up to deliver a shot that would make Pelé raise his eyebrows. I met the ball perfectly, and sent the ball screaming . . . about ten yards over the crossbar. The ball landed in the next county.

So what's the moral of the story? You don't always need to kill the ball to put it in the goal. I missed an easy scoring chance because I let my emotions dictate my actions. The power shot has merit, but only when warranted.

Perhaps you're more than twelve yards out and you have a clear shot on goal. You may want to increase your backswing and hit the ball with your laces. The technique for hitting the power shot is just like hitting a long, instep pass. What you must keep in mind, however, is that the ball must be kept under the crossbar.

Concentrate on staying over the ball when striking the power shot. Keep your knee over the ball, and don't lean back. As soon as you lean back or reach for the ball, your shot elevates much more easily.

When balls are moving toward you, you don't have to swing so hard. Focus on striking the ball with your laces and directing it to the area of intent. Shorten your backswing and follow-through and stay over the ball. You'll be surprised at how much steam you can put on it. When you have a big backswing, there is a greater margin for error because the ball is in motion.

Bending Your Shots

Great scorers make something out of nothing. With a defender in front of them and the goalkeeper positioned at the proper angle, it may appear that a good shot is not available. But bending the ball opens up a whole new set of options that can beat goalies and light up scoreboards.

It's Fair to say . . .

When I played striker as a youngster, I would try to elevate my shots and aim for the upper half of the goal. Goalkeepers at the youth level are too small to reach high shots, and it was an easy way to rack up the goals. Most young players try to hit the same shots that I did, but unfortunately, it gets you into a bad habit.

Once you advance to higher levels of play, goalies are bigger and develop better leaping ability. Those high shots aren't out of their reach anymore and are actually easier saves to make. Catching balls up near your face is a natural reaction. It's almost like self-defense. Your hands are much quicker moving up. In addition, aiming for the upper part of the goal runs the risk of shooting the ball over the goal.

It's better to keep the ball low when you shoot. It forces the keeper to make a save. Balls that are down and to the side are the toughest shots to handle. They have to go down and get it. Also, there is a chance of a rebound if the goalie mishandles the ball, enabling anyone who is following the shot to finish.

The ability to bend a ball is critical when striking restarts.

Bending the ball means you strike it so it curves during flight. This is accomplished by hitting the ball slightly off center with the inside or outside of your foot (as explained in Chapter 4). In all, you have four options to bend the ball. Strike the ball with the outside of your right foot or inside of your left to bend the ball from left to right, and strike the ball with the outside of your left or inside of your right to bend the ball from right to left.

Taking a direct kick from twenty-five yards or closer is a perfect example of when to bend the ball. Naturally, the defense will build a wall, allowing the goalie to focus on defending the far post. The wall protects the near post.

Let's say the foul occurred on the left side of the field, four yards outside the penalty box. The keeper will align the wall to cover the left side of the goal (the near post), while she stands in the net just off the right side of the ball to defend the far post. As the shooter, by striking the ball with the outside of the right foot or inside of the left, you can start the ball out around the left side of the wall so it bends into the corner of the near post. The goalie will have a difficult time saving the shot, because she's depending on her wall to cover the near post and she's on the other side of the goal.

You can also bend your shot in traffic or when the goalie has come out of the goal to reduce your shooting angle. Strike the ball with the side of your foot so you can start it out away from her and then watch it curl inside the post.

The more off center you strike the ball, the more spin (and bend) you impart on the ball. Your shot will travel slower, but when it nestles into the corner of the goal, it's a thing of beauty.

Volley Shots

Connecting with a volley shot makes for some pretty exciting soccer. If you've hit a volley on the sweet spot and scored, you've felt that sense of exhilaration. It's almost like, "Did I just do that?"

Simply stated, a volley is striking a ball out of the air with your foot. A successful volley shot entails two separate functions of execution: timing and technique. You can't have one without the other. Your technique can be picture perfect, but if you don't time the shot correctly, nothing prosperous will transpire from your efforts. Great timing but poor technique will also be fruitless. Each element is equally essential to putting the ball on goal.

Here is my advice as it pertains to timing. Practice. And when you're finished practicing, practice some more. I know, I'm starting to sound like a broken record, but it's the only way to develop timing. There are no shortcuts. Timing is not just about gauging the speed of the ball but also about synchronizing all of your body movements that build up to the physical act of striking a volley. Accomplishing this takes repetitious training. Imagine asking your dad to volley a soccer ball. Do you know why that image just brought a smile to your face? Because you're thinking about how discombobulated your father would look trying to kick a ball out of the air. In your father's defense, he's had no practice volleying shots, and, as a result, he has no timing or technique.

Practice three types of volleys: the full volley, the half volley, and the side volley. With each shot, the instep (laces of your shoes) is used to strike the ball. When executed correctly, they all produce explosive shots that overwhelm goalkeepers.

Full volley shot. A full volley shot is used when the ball is coming directly at you. The important thing to remember is to be patient. The most common mistake players make is that they don't allow the ball to get low enough.

They greet the ball with their foot too early, producing a shot that's cranked over the goal. Let the ball drop, so you strike it just before it hits the ground. Keep your eyes glued to the ball the entire way. Because you already know where the goal is, your eyes have no reason to look anywhere but at the ball.

Use a short, compact backswing on volley shots. It increases your chances of striking the ball solidly. The speed of the ball coming at you will generate velocity on your shot, so a huge backswing is unnecessary. Keep your stroke short and powerful.

Track the ball all the way into your foot, and strike it with your laces. Lean over the ball as you strike it to keep your shot low. Leaning back makes the ball elevate. You'll know when you've hit a front volley right because there is visible topspin. Often, the ball will escalate quickly but then dip down under the crossbar because of the topspin.

Finish the shot by following through. Land on your kicking foot and get ready to celebrate!

Half volleys. A half volley is when you strike the ball just after it hits the ground. Use the same technique as employed for a full volley shot, and make sure your body stays over the ball.

A ball struck along the ground to the side of goalie is one of the toughest shots to stop.

When striking a full volley shot, let the ball get down. Keep your upper body over the ball and punch it with your laces.

Exercise patience to allow the ball to hit the ground, and strike it immediately after it lands. It's a timing issue that requires practice, so put in the necessary practice time and reap the benefits during competition.

Side volleys. A side volley is used to strike a ball out of the air when it's coming toward you at an angle (not straight on). Side volleys necessitate precision timing and perfect technique. It's a tough shot, but when you pull it off, it's truly a work of art.

Hitting a half volley requires you to strike the ball immediately after it hits the ground. Keep your knee over the ball and your head down.

When striking a side volley, your body is going to be more horizontal instead of vertical. Focus on kicking the upper half of the ball so it goes downward. For the sake of simple explanation, let's say the ball is crossed from the right side of the field.

Stay on your toes to adjust your positioning until it's time to shoot. (Often, you'll have to reposition yourself as the ball is in flight to execute this shot.) Take a short backswing, and drop your left shoulder to make your body parallel to the ground. Strike downward through the top half of the ball, and finish by landing on your kicking foot.

Framing the Goal

Framing the goal is performed by nonshooting attackers who run forward to the outside of the goalposts as a shot is taken. By positioning themselves two or three yards outside the posts, you extend the width of the goal on the shot. If a shot is traveling wide of the goal and you time it right, you can be right there to redirect the ball into the net. If the ball is deflected by the goalkeeper or caroms off the post, you're there to tap it in. Players can make a living out of framing the goal.

Notice that I dip my left shoulder before striking a side volley with my right foot (top). It allows me to get my foot on a parallel plane with the ball. After you strike the ball, follow through and land on your kicking foot (above).

It's Fair to say . . .

From very close range, say from six yards and in, use the inside of your foot to redirect a cross. It provides a broader surface to strike the ball and requires a much shorter backswing.

A hard shot in this situation is not necessary unless you are more comfortable striking the ball with your laces. When the ball is crossed, the goalie will be scrambling to gain position. On the move, she'll be unable to set, meaning your job is to simply put the ball on goal. Blind luck is the only chance she has to make a save. Use the inside of your foot to knock the ball home, and then go thank your teammate for setting you up for an easy score.

on every shot, because the moment you don't, the ball will pop out to the spot you should have been.

At UNC, we'd run shooting drills and actually practice framing the goal. Players who

Scoring consistently by framing the goal is not luck. It's a combination of hustle, discipline, and intuitiveness. At UNC, Debbie Keller was the best at framing the goal. She scored so many goals that way because she sensed where to be, when to be there, and most important, she was always there. Never did she assume the keeper would make a clean save. She framed the goal every time, and it paid big dividends for her. It's important that you frame the goal

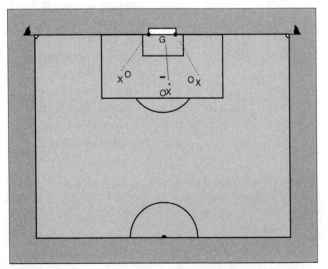

FIGURE 6.1
As the player takes a shot (middle X), her teammates should immediately run to the outside of the posts to frame the goal.

It's Almost Unfair

Many point to the UCLA men's basketball team as having the greatest dynasty in the history of collegiate sports. From 1964 to 1975, the Bruins won ten out of twelve national NCAA championships, which included a run of seven straight (1967 through 1973). After checking out these numbers from the UNC women's soccer program, sports fans might want to reconsider their opinion.

YEAR	RECORD	PERCENTAGE	
*1979	10–2–0	0.833	
*1980	21–5–0	0.807	
1981	23–0–0	1.000	(national champion)
1982	19–2–0	0.905	(national champion)
1983	19–1–0	0.950	(national champion)
1984	24–0–1	0.980	(national champion)
1985	18–2–1	0.881	(national runner-up)
1986	24–0–1	0.980	(national champion)
1987	23–0–1	0.979	(national champion)
1988	18–0–3	0.929	(national champion)
1989	24–0–1	0.980	(national champion)
1990	20–1–1	0.932	(national champion)
1991	24–0–0	1.000	(national champion)
1992	25–0–0	1.000	(national champion)
1993	23–0–0	1.000	(national champion)
1994	25–1–1	0.944	(national champion)
1995	25–1–0	0.962	(tied for third place)
1996	25–1–0	0.962	(national champion)
1997	27–0–1	0.982	(national champion)
1998	25–1–0	0.962	(national runner-up)
1999	24–2–0	0.923	(national champion)
2000	21–3–0	0.875	(national champion)
2001	24–1–0	0.960	(national runner-up)

Overall record: 511–23–11

ACC regular season record: 75–4–1

NCAA Tournament Record: 71–4–0

Career goals for: 2,365

Career goals against: 244

* no national champion recognized for women's soccer

were waiting in line to shoot would stand off the goalpost. If the ball is hit wide, we would redirect the shot on goal. Anson thought deflecting and redirecting shots should be treated as a skill or special craft. I guarantee through the course of a Carolina soccer season, many goals will be scored as a result of framing the goal.

Be sure not to overrun the goalposts when framing. If you do that, you're not framing anything. If you run too close to the post, a ball that pops out will extend outside of your reach and scoot past you. Get to a spot that's a couple yards off the goal line. Sprint to a spot outside the posts, and then break down your steps to react to the ball. In the game, one of the goals I set for myself when playing forward is to frame the goal on every shot. A scoring opportunity might present itself or it might not, but you can bet I'll be there if it does.

Drills

Just the Two of Us

The wall is your best friend when practicing your skills. In this drill, you'll need a wall, some white or black tape, and your little buddy (the soccer ball).

With a piece of tape, mark two spots on the wall that are twenty-four feet apart. This is the width of the goal. The markings should be low on the wall near the ground. Next, place a piece of tape two yards in from each side of the markings. This creates a left-hand corner and a right-hand corner.

Starting from approximately ten yards away from the wall, try to hit the wall in the corner spots marked by the tape. Practice striking the ball with both feet. Also use the inside, instep, and outside of your feet. Hit the ball as it is moving (to create a gamelike situation) or strike it off the dribble. Gradually move back to increase the distance of your shots.

To keep track of your shooting accuracy, take ten shots with each foot from ten, fourteen, eighteen, and twenty-two yards away. Record how many shots hit the corners and try to beat your score the next time out. This way you can create competition when there is none. When I compete with myself, I'm one of the most difficult opponents I've ever had!

Placement for Points

Here is a game that forces you to concentrate on shooting the ball accurately. You'll need a soccer goal, four cones, and four balls. Grab a group of teammates for some fun-loving competition.

Place two cones along the goal line. Position one cone a yard (three feet) inside the left post and the other cone a yard inside the right post. Place the second set of cones two yards in from the first set. (The second set of cones is nine feet from the goalposts.)

Here is the point system. Any ball that crosses the goal line between the posts and the first set of cones is worth three points. Balls that cross between the first and second set of cones are worth two points. Balls crossing inside the second set of cones (through the middle of the goal) are worth one point.

Each competitor takes four shots. The first two are off the dribble. The first shot is from the top of the circle and the second shot is from the eighteen-yard line. For the third shot, a ground pass is given to the shooter standing at the penalty mark (twelve-yard line). She must use a first-time strike. The final shot is a penalty kick. The player who tallies the most points wins.

To spice up the game, extend the game to three rounds. During the first round, shooters must kick the ball with the side of the foot. The second-round shots are struck with the outside of the foot, and the final-round shots are hit with the instep.

Make sure you include both feet!

Rapid Fire

This exercise is a lot of fun because you get to take a variety of shots in a short period of time. You'll need three teammates, four soccer balls, and a goal for this drill.

To start, all your teammates are on the left side of the field. Each has a soccer ball. Player 1 is standing at the eighteen-yard line on the left side of the semicircle. Player 2 is standing on the line making the penalty box area (on the left side) approximately eight yards from the end line. Player 3 is set up for a corner kick. You're positioned (with a ball) in the middle of the field approximately twenty-five yards from the goal.

On the coach's whistle, strike your ball on goal as if it were a direct kick. Player 1 then sends a ground pass across the eighteen-yard line. Use a first-time strike. Continue to move forward where you'll receive an aerial pass (around the eight-yard line) from player 2. Volley a shot out of the air. Finally, run to the far post to knock in a headball off a corner kick from player 3. Are you out of breath yet?

Rotate with your teammates so everyone gets a turn from each position. When the cycle is completed, flip everyone to the right side of the field and start over.

"I think the best goalies are ones

who are fearless, intuitive,

and exude impenetrable confidence."

Goalkeeping

When I think of goalkeepers, I think of the eccentric one in the group. I don't know what it is, but it always seems like the goalie position attracts the most colorful personality on the team. I think they all have their own little sorority, where quirky traits and unpredictable behavior patterns are a prerequisite to earn membership.

Don't get me wrong. I love goalies. Not to mention that they can save your butt if your mark gets behind you and rips an open shot on net. Obviously, goalies can be the difference between a win and a loss.

Soccer Player First— Goalkeeper Second

As you know, the goalie is the only player on the team permitted to use her hands. Goalkeepers use their hands in a variety of ways. They can catch, tip, punch, field, or toss the ball with their hands during any time that the ball is within their own penalty area. That said, goalkeepers must develop their soccer skills just like the rest of their teammates. Throughout a season, there will be countless situations where the goalie must kick a ball rolling toward her, trap a ball that's passed back to her, deliver a pass to her teammate, or even make a tackle.

At practice, participate in skill exercises along with your teammates. Work in passing and receiving drills, dribbling drills, tackling drills, and so forth. Develop comfort having the ball at your feet. It's a critical aspect to becoming a complete goalkeeper. I've seen far too many goals scored because a goalkeeper lacked the ability to receive the ball with control, made an errant pass, or simply lost possession because her touch was erratic. Think of yourself as a soccer player first and a goalkeeper second.

A Vocal Leader

Goalkeepers *must* talk on the field. I can't stress enough how important it is for goalies to be vocal on the field and give direction to their

Goalkeeping isn't limited to making acrobatic saves. You've got to be a field general as well.

teammates. Even when the ball is outside of your defensive third of the field, the goalie should be orchestrating teammates from her post.

Have you ever seen the movie *Pulp Fiction*? In one scene, Uma Thurman and John Travolta talk about "comfortable silence." They say that if you can spend time with your date or significant other and sit in silence without feeling uncomfortable, then you know you are compatible. I agree with that on a personal level, but on the soccer field, there is no such thing as a "comfortable silence." If a ball is crossed near the goalmouth and I hear absolutely nothing from my goalkeeper, it's the most uncomfortable feeling in the world.

As the goalie, you have the best view of the field. You can see what each offensive player is doing, when and where they're making their runs, what the ball handler sees, and where all of your defensive teammates are positioned. It's your responsibility to alert the defense if a player is unmarked, if an opposing defender is making a through run out of the backfield, or if a forward has gotten goal-side. Being vocal is not limited to calling for the ball. You've got to be a field general for your team.

Part of being a goalkeeper is making judgments. Do I come out to intercept a cross? Should I run out to play a ball that has rolled into the penalty area? Whatever you decide to do, you must commit 100 percent to the decision, and let everyone know what you're doing. You can't be timid or apprehensive.

Once you decide to do something, call it out with confidence. If I'm playing defense and hear the goalie call out in a wavering tone, I become nervous. I may try to take matters into my own hands if I detect apprehension in the goalkeeper's voice. Support your decision and sound self-assured. A poor decision is understandable, but one that lacks confidence diminishes the trust your teammates have in your ability.

The Fundamentals of Goalkeeping

When I'm playing defense, I like to think that if our defensive unit plays well enough, we could win the game with my Uncle Bob in goal. (No offense, Uncle Bob, but I've seen your vertical leap. You can barely slide a piece of paper under your feet.) But seriously, even with a great defense playing in the backfield, the goalkeeper will be tested. Shots and crosses travel at different velocities from various angles. The ball may have spin, which affects its flight pattern, and all strikes are hit to varying locations. Most of the spectacular saves can be attributed to exceptional instinct and athletic ability. But the ordinary saves, the ones that you'll make 90 percent of the time, are made by using proper technique. Master the basics to defend your goal.

Goalie Stance: The Ready Position

When a ball handler gets into a position where she's a threat to shoot, square your shoulders to the shooter and lock onto her with both eyes. Point your toes at the shooter, and spread your feet no farther than shoulder-width apart. Flex your knees and bend slightly forward at the waist. Hold your hands down at your sides with your palms facing the ball. Center your weight on the balls of your feet and lean slightly forward. Oh yeah . . . and relax.

A common mistake that goalkeepers make is that they spread their feet too far apart. Positioning your feet outside of your shoulder line is a typical stance for a basketball player playing defense or a tennis player awaiting a serve, but it should not be employed in the goal. It inhibits your ability to jump, making you susceptible to high shots. Try jumping up as high as you can right now. The first thing you'll do is move your feet closer together. In goal, you may not have enough time to shuffle your feet in. You'll either be late with your jump or sacrifice height on your vertical leap. Either way, you're in trouble. Start with your feet shoulder-width apart to eliminate a potential weakness.

If the attacker is shooting from very close range, lower your center of gravity. Bend deeper at the knees and lean forward. The ball will

My Philadelphia Charge teammate Janel Schilling is set in the ready position.

have less time to elevate from a close distance, so chances are the shot will be low. Move your hands out away from your sides (palms facing the ball) and creep forward a step or two to reduce the shooter's angle. This puts you in good position to react to a close-range shot.

Cutting Down the Shooter's Angle

Playing goal is not just about quick feet and great hands. It also takes a little something upstairs to succeed—a little brain activity. Where you position yourself is just as important as how you position yourself to set up a save. Minimizing angles and adjusting your depth will not only make you a better keeper but will make your job easier as well.

On shots taken from the right side of the field, move to your left to reduce the shooter's angle.

Let's say the ball handler is coming down the right side of the field (to your left). Do you want to remain in the middle of the goal? Absolutely not. By staying in the middle, the shooter has the option of hitting the ball to the near post (to your left) or the far post (to your right). You want to take away one of those options. Shuffle your feet to the left to eliminate her shot to the near post. Square your shoulders to the shooter and set in the ready position.

Established goalkeepers often cheat a little when cutting down angles. This is done one of two ways. The first is to slide over far enough so that the shooter has no space to shoot the ball between the keeper and the near post. By doing this, she can lean slightly to her right in anticipation of a shot to the far post. The second way to cheat is to allow a little bit of space between the keeper and the near post. This allows her to cover more ground toward the far post (to your right). Most shooters automatically aim for the far post in this situation, but keep in mind that there is some room to sneak a ball past you to the near post.

Always respect the player with the ball. She poses a serious threat on the field. If a player has the ball deep to the side and has an extremely difficult angle to shoot on goal, don't assume she'll cross the ball and come off your nearside post. Smart players will take advantage if you anticipate too quickly. They'll rip a shot from a seemingly impossible angle, and before you know what happened, you'll be collecting the ball out of the back of the net. Keep your weight balanced in the middle until you see the shot.

Reduce the angle with depth. What can you do if the shooter is right smack in the middle of the field? If you move to the right or left, you give her a greater goal area to one side. The answer is to come off your line. Take steps out toward the shooter to reduce her shooting lanes.

Ready for a quick geometry lesson? Let's say the goalposts and the shooter represent the points of a triangle. The goal line is the base of the triangle, and the shooter represents the apex of the triangle. The shooter strikes a ball to your right toward the corner. If you're standing along the goal line, you have to travel the maximum distance to your right to stop the shot. But if you had come out a few feet (off your line), you could intercept the ball before it reaches its maximum width (the corner of the goal). You've reduced the distance you have to move laterally to make the save.

Coming out of the goal, however, does have some drawbacks. First, the closer you are to the shooter, the less time you have to react. You may minimize the lateral distance you have to cover, but a hard shot will be on you much quicker. Second, you're now susceptible to chip shots aimed toward the upper part of the goal. If a player notices you coming out, she may attempt to loft the ball over your head. This is a very difficult shot to execute, which reduces the risk factor. But don't come out too far. Accurate shooters will make you pay. Again, use your good judgment.

If a shot is being taken from the middle of the field, get off your line to limit the shooter's goal area (from side to side).

Catching the Ball

When a shot is taken on goal, your primary objective is to keep the ball from crossing the goal line. Your secondary objective is to catch and control the ball. How you catch the ball depends on its vertical and horizontal path of flight, but one aspect of the save remains constant. Whenever possible, get your body behind the ball. If the shot is to your right and you have time, shuffle your feet to the right so that your body is centered behind the ball. If the ball happens to slip through your hands, or takes a bad hop off the ground, your body will block the ball from getting past you.

Fielding shots off the ground. Shots that travel along the ground appear to be the most harmless, but if you don't field them properly, the results can be disastrous. I think that because the ball is rolling, a goalkeeper might sometimes allow her thoughts to move ahead to what she's going to do with the ball once she receives it. Her eyes glance upward to take a peek upfield to identify an outlet. Before she knows it, the ball is mishandled and rebounds to a forward framing the goal and she taps it in for an easy score. Shots on the ground present

just as much danger as any other shot. As long as it's on net, it's a threat that deserves your full attention. Focus on executing the proper technique.

To field the ball, move your feet so the ball arrives within the frame of your body. Try to set up so that you are centered behind the ball. Spread your feet out so they're positioned wider than shoulder-width. Drop your weak-side foot slightly back, so that the strong-side foot is planted slightly ahead. (If you move to right, your left foot is your weak-side foot.) Bend at the knees and lower your rear end. Lean forward with your upper body, and reach out for the ball.

Place your hands on the ground with your palms facing upward. Rotate your hands slightly inward so the ball is funneled in toward your midsection. As the ball approaches, extend your fingers toward the bottom half of the ball. Keep your eyes locked on the ball as it rolls onto your fingers. With your shoulders hunched forward, scoop the ball up into your chest with two hands.

When fielding shots off the ground, reach for the ball and watch it all the way into your hands.

The number-one mistake goalkeepers make is they take their eyes off the ball too early. They rise up out of their position prematurely, which causes them to juggle or completely miss the ball. Also, goalkeepers forget to lower their rear end. They only flex their knees and bend down at the waist. Keep your rear end down and eyes on the ball.

Keys to Catching the Ground Shot
- Get your body behind the ball.

- Bend at the knees and lower your rear end.

- Reach out for the ball.

- Watch the ball roll into your hands!

The scoop catch. The scoop catch is used when balls are traveling off the ground but below your chest. This is a tough save, as goalies are often caught "in between."

For aerial shots hit below your chest, move your feet toward the ball's line of flight. Square your shoulders to the ball, and lean forward at the waist. Lower your upper body bending at the knees. How much you bend depends on the height of the shot. Your objective is to get your chest behind the ball.

Leaning slightly forward at the waist, extend both arms with the palms facing upward. Push your elbows inward, and make sure they are slightly bent (or flexed). As you receive the shot, curl your arms upward and trap the ball against your chest. Keep your head down and eyes locked on the ball the entire time.

Surround the ball with your arms to ensure control. On awkward shots or shots that move or knuckle, take a slight jump backwards as you receive the ball to give it some cushion. Raise your knee up after catching the ball to secure and protect it from incoming attackers.

On very low shots, it may be necessary to drop to your knees to make a scoop catch. If the ball is hit hard and traveling at you at or just

Curl your body around the ball when making a scoop catch.

above your shins, quickly drop down to your knees. After receiving the ball, fall forward onto the ground and curl around the ball for protection.

The diamond catch. This is my favorite type of catch. Anything that has the word *diamond* in its title is a winner in my book. Hear that, boys?

When a shot is traveling chest or head high, use the diamond technique to make the save. To execute, hold your arms straight out in front of you. Extend your hands as if you were telling someone to stop. Tilt your hands inward and bring them together so that your thumbs and pointer fingers are touching. The space formed by your fingers touching should be in the shape of a diamond. I know, it's not quite as glamorous as you had hoped, but it's a start!

Get your body in the line with the shot, with your shoulders square to the ball. Extend your arms out in front of you, and then draw them toward you slightly so you have some give when

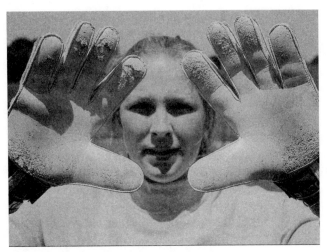

The hand position for the diamond catch. That is one huge diamond Janel is outlining.

you catch the ball. Receive the ball in the middle of the diamond, wrap your fingers around the ball, and bring it directly in toward your chest. Fold your arms around the ball to secure it.

It's important to reach out with your hands to catch the ball. That way, your eyes can track the ball right into your fingertips. If your hands are held in near your chest, your eyes may lose sight of the ball, and you'll have trouble

Catch the ball out in front with the pads of your fingers when making a diamond catch. It allows you some room for cushion and to see the ball all the way into your hands.

catching it cleanly. Think of an Olympic marksman holding her rifle. She doesn't aim the rifle holding it down near her midsection. She extends it out in front of her so her eyes can look down the line. It's the same idea when making a diamond catch.

Diving Saves

Occasionally, you don't have time to get your body behind the ball. Close-range shots and zingers pinged toward the corner pocket of the net may leave you with only one option to make the save, and that is to leave your feet and dive. (A zinger is a hard shot and pinging the ball is hitting a hard shot.)

Like many save techniques, how you dive depends on the location of the shot. Low shots to the side, midlevel shots far to either side, and shots driven toward the upper 90 of the goal all require different methods of diving. The following is a description of each type.

The collapse dive. The collapse dive is generally used for low shots that are hit from close range. The ball is only a foot or two to either side. The term collapse stems from the fact that your upper body sort of just drops to the side of the ball.

To describe this save, let's say the ball is kicked to your right. From a narrow stance, kick your right foot to the left, in front of your left leg. Hold your right arm down by your side about a foot wide of your waist, palm facing out. As your right foot kicks, drop your right shoulder down. Allow gravity to take over and let your left foot leave the ground. Your body should collapse down to the right.

With your eyes following the shot, stop the ball with your right hand, and, if possible, cradle the ball inward to gain control. Raise your left knee upward to a crunch position to protect the ball. This same technique is used on shots hit to your left.

Ronnie Fair

Twin sister

"Part of Lorrie's success can be attributed to her being such a focused person. If she wants something, she takes the most direct route. She goes from point A to point B. I get easily distracted. I take the route that appears to be the most interesting. I guess that's why I'm the left-handed one."

Laying out: full extension dives. These are the diving saves that will put you on ESPN's "SportsCenter." A laser shot is ripped to a corner, and you lay out (full extension) to grab the ball and prevent a goal. The shooter snarls at you, and your defenders pump their fists in excitement.

Diving saves mean more than just keeping a goal off the scoreboard. They can act as a momentum shifter in a game. Great shots or

Even when you dive, it's important to keep your eyes focused on the ball.

good scoring opportunities don't come along that often throughout a contest, and if the offense executes perfectly only to find their attempt thwarted by a spectacular save, it can really take the wind out of their sails.

We'll say this shot is hit to your left. Take a step to the side and slightly forward with your left foot. Your stride should be as long as possible but only as long as time permits. The sooner you have to dive, the shorter your stride will be. The right foot simply follows along with the left.

Your left hand leads the dive. Reach out to the left with your palm facing the ball. As your arm extends, your lower body follows by pushing off the lead foot. Direct your dive to the left and slightly forward. Reach across your body with your right hand, extending over the plane of the ball to form a window for your eyes to track the shot.

At the peak of your dive, your body is parallel to the ground. Your objective is to catch the ball with your hands. Once the ball is secure in your grip, rotate your hands inward. This helps you maintain control of the ball when you hit the ground.

Once you hit the ground, pull your arms (and the ball) in toward your midsection. Raise your knees into a crunched position to protect yourself and the ball from attackers. Forwards tend to get pretty angry when a keeper makes a diving save, so if they see there is even a chance to knock the ball loose, they'll attack.

Catching the ball cleanly is not always a possibility. You may only be able to get your fingers on the ball. If this is the case, firm up your fingers as the ball hits your hand. Limp fingers may not stop the ball from hitting the back of the net. After making the save, react quickly. Either pounce on the ball immediately if it's close to you, or scramble to your feet as fast as possible to set up for a second shot. A great save is only worth its weight in gold if you can muster up enough savvy to deny the follow-up shot.

On high shots sent to your left, turn counter-clockwise, leap off of your left foot, and push the ball over the crossbar with your right hand (left). If the ball is hit directly at you, jump off the leg of your choice and parry the shot with your fingertips (right).

Parrying high shots. There will be times when you'll be able to leap up and snare a high shot right out of the air, but other times the ball will be too high to catch. In this case, you'll have to parry the shot. Parrying a shot simply means tipping it or redirecting a shot over the goal.

There are two methods of parrying a shot. The first is when the ball is hit high and to your side, and the second is when the ball is hit high directly above you.

On balls hit to either side, turn your body away from the shot. On a ball hit high to your right, rotate your body clockwise so that your left shoulder points to the ball. Bend slightly at the knees and leap up off your right leg. Follow the ball with your eyes and extend your near-

side arm (in this case your left arm) to the ball. Raise your fingers up to reach the highest possible level. Push your palm up into the underside of the ball to redirect its path upward. When your palm intersects with the momentum of the ball, it will carom over the crossbar. "She makes the save!"

For shots hit directly above you, stay square to the ball. Jump up off of one leg. (Usually, there is one leg that you would prefer to jump off of, so use that one. It's usually the leg you're most comfortable using when shooting a lay-up in basketball.) Lift the opposite-side knee up, and parry the shot with the opposite-side hand. If you jump off your right leg, make the save with your left hand.

Handling High Crosses

Aerial balls that are served into the box are always dangerous scoring threats. As a goalkeeper, the first thing you need to do is make a decision. Whether the ball is crossed from the side off the dribble, struck off a corner kick, or served from the midfield, you've got to commit yourself to going after the ball or holding your ground to guard the goal. There can be no apprehension on your part, especially if you decide to play the ball.

There are two techniques of playing the ball off a high cross. You can catch the ball using the diamond catch method, or you can punch the ball away from danger. In general, catch the ball if you can get to it easily. But if it's a crowded area and a plausible risk is involved, punch it out of there. Dropping the ball or getting beat to it by an opposing player can result in allowing a goal.

The key element when catching or punching a high cross is to time your jump to intercept the ball at your highest point of reach. When the ball is very high, you boast an advantage over the field players because you can extend your arms and use your hands. Once the ball is at a point you can reach it, go after it like a shark in the water.

When you leave the ground, jump off of one leg and square your shoulders to the direction of the ball (whenever possible). If you're catching the ball, flex your elbows (if possible) so you can give with the ball as you catch. Upon receipt, tuck the ball in toward your chest to ensure possession and control. When punching the ball, square your shoulders and punch it back in the direction it came from. Use both fists with your thumbs facing inward. Draw your hands back, and punch it at its pinnacle point. Aim for the middle of the ball, and punch through it. To increase height, hit lower on the ball.

Exercising good judgment is critical when playing high crosses. To improve judgment, take as many balls as possible during practice. It's the only way to get better. With time, your decisions will become instinctive and allow you to get to more balls.

Delivering the Ball

You've positioned yourself perfectly by cutting down the angle of the shot. You got into your keeper position and fielded the shot with fundamental precision. Your teammates breathe a sigh of relief and now shift their focus to transition. So now what? You've made the save, and all of a sudden you're standing there with the ball in your hands.

Distributing the ball is a crucial aspect of playing goal. Goalkeepers who make good decisions serve as a bonus weapon to their team's offensive arsenal. There are four basic methods of delivering the ball once it's in your hands. You can roll the ball, use an overhand toss, punt it, or send a drop kick. Each has its place and should be practiced regularly.

The roll. The roll is a lot like your sister's fifth-grade birthday party. You're bowling for dollars.

In a crowd of players, use both fists and punch the ball out of danger.

The technique is nearly identical, except of course that there are no holes in a soccer ball. If you throw right-handed, stride toward the target with your left foot. Draw your right arm back with the ball in the palm of your hand. Bend deep at the knees and release the ball as it passes your stride foot.

Rolls are generally used for short outlet passes to defenders. Once the goalkeeper secures the ball, opposing players often drop back in anticipation of a punt. The goalie can then simply roll the ball to a teammate to ensure possession.

If you're up near the eighteen-yard line, roll passes can also be used to quickly deliver a ball to a player running upfield into space.

The most accurate way to distribute the ball is to roll it. Rolling also provides the receiver with the easiest ball to handle. It's limited to short distance passes but provides a quick method of distribution.

Roll the ball when making a quick outlet pass.

Overhand toss. At times, you will want to quickly get the ball to a player upfield. In this case, use an overhand toss. You'll be able to generate more distance and velocity on your throws and can quickly get things moving.

An overhand toss is different from a baseball (or softball) throw. Because a soccer ball is big, it's difficult to guarantee accuracy. The ball can slip out of your hand or roll off to one side.

When using the overhand toss, cup the ball in your hand. You're not going to throw the ball as much as you're going to sling it down field. Step directly toward your target with your left foot (assuming you're right-handed), and tilt your shoulders upward. Draw your arm back and down to load up for power. As your stride foot hits the ground, pull your left arm in toward your midsection and fire the ball overhand at your target. The ball should roll off your fingertips upon release, imparting backspin on the ball. Backspin allows the ball to carry better through the air.

It's important to follow through when using the overhand toss. Don't cut your release short, because it will diminish the distance and velocity of your toss. Complete the throw by finishing with your right arm draped over your left leg.

The punt. The punt is used to boot the ball downfield. One of our pregame goals as a team is to win every punt out of the air. Punts quickly transport the ball out of your defensive end and into your attacking third.

Punting the ball effectively is an issue of timing and concentration. I think most miskicked punts are caused by a lack of focus. To perfect your timing and consistently strike the ball solid, practice punting over and over.

Punts are struck with the instep of your foot. As you take your final step to punt the ball, draw your kicking leg back and drop the ball just in front of you. Do not toss the ball high up in the air. This is a common mistake made by young goalies and increases the chances of a

To toss the ball, hold the ball in the palm of your hand, take a step toward your target, and tilt your shoulders upward (left). Stiffen your plant leg, shift your weight forward, and fire the ball from a high release point (right).

To elevate your punts, lean slightly backward before contact.

miskick. Hold the ball up near your waist as you take your steps and drop it to your kicking foot side. Strike the ball just before it hits the ground.

As you kick the ball, lean back so your foot strikes the bottom of the ball. This elevates the ball and also avoids applying too much topspin. When the ball leaves your foot with a lot of topspin, it will quickly dip or dive and minimize distance. Leaning forward as you punt the ball will produce mediocre results at best.

The drop kick. Another craft that requires great timing, drop kicks are effective when kicking into the wind. The ball travels on a low trajectory and cuts through wind resistance. In addition, if struck correctly, you can impart backspin on the ball, which allows it to carry much better than a punt. Regardless of the weather, goalies who master the art of drop kicking can send the ball a long, long way.

Drop kicks are similar to half volleys. Let the ball hit the ground and immediately strike it afterward. When facing a strong wind, use the drop kick to send the ball on a low trajectory to maximize distance.

Similar to the punt, drop the ball to the ground as you take your final step. The ball is dropped slightly earlier than you would when executing a punt. Your kicking foot strikes the ball immediately after it hits the ground. The ball is actually traveling on its way up as it's hit and, if you catch it right, will be driven with backspin.

As mentioned, use this method of distribution when facing strong winds. It's the only chance you have of getting sufficient length on your kicks.

The Breakaway: Everything to Gain

A breakaway is one of the most exciting plays in soccer. Forwards dream of getting this opportunity during the game, and, as a confident goalkeeper, you should relish the challenge as well.

When confronted by a one-on-one breakaway, the number-one point to keep in mind is that the pressure is on the attacker. Everyone expects her to score in this situation. You simply play the role of the spoiler. This mindset allows you to vigorously pursue the play and maintain an "everything to gain, nothing to lose" attitude. Americans love playing the underdog in sports, and, in this case, you're the underdog.

The key to defending the goal in a breakaway situation is to be aggressive. Take the action to the striker. If the forward is running on to a through ball, your job is to get the ball as soon as possible. You can get to the ball before the attacker, get to it before the attacker shoots, play the ball as the attacker shoots, or play it just after she shoots. Notice that there aren't any options that have you waiting near the goal line. To have a chance at making the save, you've got to leave your post and minimize the goal area that the striker has to place her shot.

Allow the play to dictate your speed. For example, if you have a chance to reach the ball before the striker, turn up the throttle and race out to the ball. Conversely, if the attacker has the ball at her feet, come out gradually and maintain control of your body. You must be able to leave your feet at any time. Don't come out like gangbusters, because she'll easily slip the ball past you or dribble around you and into an open net (my personal favorite). The best way to approach it is each time she touches the ball to dribble, move forward. If she's dribbling, she can't be shooting, and you can safely move out to reduce her angle.

To make a save, dive parallel to the ground, and stretch your body as far as possible. Your hands should cover the near-post side, and your legs extend toward the far-post side. Don't simply reach out with your hands. Get your legs up

When faced with a one-on-one breakaway, you've got to come out and challenge the shooter. Take the action to her and force her to commit to a direction.

and out. Strikers like to keep the ball away from the keeper's hands and will often shoot to the far-post side. Use your feet to reduce the shooter's goal area.

Practice defending breakaways with a friend. Have her come from all different angles at varying speeds. Through trial and error, you'll begin to recognize which approach works and which fails to get the job done. Making saves in practice will be tougher than they are in the game. By adding the pressure of a live contest, the advantage goes to the keeper. You've got everything to gain and nothing to lose.

Drills

Soft Hands

Good goalkeepers have soft hands. Hands of stone cause bobbles and rebounds. To develop soft hands, practice this two-part drill.

Position yourself on the goal line with a coach or teammate standing approximately eight yards away from you. Hold one hand behind your back. Your partner should throw the ball to your free-hand side. (If your left hand is behind your back, balls should be thrown to your right hand.)

Attempt to catch the ball with one hand. To do this, reach for the ball and give with it as you catch. Because you don't have your second hand to secure the ball, you are forced to be delicate with your free hand and take the speed off the ball. After ten throws, switch hands.

For the second stage of the drill, use both hands to catch the ball. Have your partner throw balls to your left and right. Shuffle your feet to get your body centered behind the ball. Reach for the ball and give with it as you catch it. Exaggerate the movement of absorbing the shock. Keep your eyes on the ball at all times.

As you progress, ask your partner to increase the speed of her tosses. In time, you'll soften your hands and improve between the posts.

Reaction Jackson

Proper technique is important to successful goalkeeping, but reaction time is an element that further enhances keeper ability.

You'll need a partner for this drill. Stand in front of a wall with your partner approximately ten yards directly in front of you. With a ball placed at the feet of your partner, turn your back to the ball and face the wall.

The job of the server is to kick the ball at you or slightly to the left or right of you. As she approaches the ball, she yells "Turn!" just before she kicks it. You quickly turn around and attempt to make the catch.

It's important that the server keeps the ball close. If she kicks the ball too far to your right or left, it becomes too difficult to catch the ball. To raise the level of difficulty, have the server increase the velocity of her shots.

In the Line of Fire

Have the entire team (or as many players as are available) spread out across the goalmouth approximately eight yards from the goal line. Each player should be lined up with a ball at her feet. The goalkeeper minds the net.

Starting from left to right (or from the shooter's perspective right to left), the first player in line fires a hard shot at the keeper. Immediately after the first ball is struck, the second shooter approaches her ball and fires a shot at the keeper. This continues in succession until all the shooters have taken a shot.

The goalie must quickly shuffle her feet and react down the line. Starting from the left post, she attempts to block the first shot and quickly shuffles to her right to meet the second shot. She moves all the way across the goalmouth and attempts to block every shot taken.

"Winning headballs is a decision."

Heading

When I was younger, I was a little afraid of heading the ball. I would never shy away from it, but I really didn't like it. The problem was, the ball would go up in the air, and I'd take it right off the top of my head, which produced an instant headache. At some point, somebody told me that I was using the wrong part of my head. So on the next headball opportunity, I headed the ball with my face.

Eventually, I figured out that you're supposed to use your forehead. Once I learned that, the fear that I once harbored faded away. I realized that I had nothing to be afraid of as long as I employed the proper technique and used the right part of my head.

If you're a player who thinks heading a soccer ball merits a segment on the television show "Fear Factor," this chapter will really benefit your game. I say that because once you understand how to head the ball, you'll wonder what you were so afraid of. When you get back out on the field with that fear eliminated from your mind, you'll recognize how satisfying it is to win headballs and how much it enriches your overall game.

The Importance of Headballs

Heading is a critical aspect of soccer. Winning headballs makes a statement about you as a player and about your team. It tells the opposition that you're going to battle for every ball and do whatever it takes to gain possession. Dominating the air has a tremendous psychological effect on the other team. They'll feel as if they're being outplayed and lose confidence as you gain a psychological edge. Games can be won and lost on 50/50 balls, so consider that each time a ball takes to the air.

Winning headballs is a decision. Getting into position and having proper timing are factors, but the first step is a determination to win the ball out of the air. When you see the ball in the air, your mind should say, "That ball is mine." I'm not the tallest person out on the field nor do I have the best vertical jump, but I'm convinced I'm going to win every single headball that comes in my direction.

On deep kicks that will land behind you, run back to get behind the point of the ball's descent (left). Take a few steps forward, leap up, and head the ball at your maximum height.

What Is Gained by Using Your Head?

- An accurate form of shooting

- A quick pass that keeps play moving

- Winning those crucial 50/50 balls

- A deadly weapon on restarts

The Proper Mechanics of Heading

Exercising the proper technique for skills like dribbling, shooting, and passing improves accuracy, power, and consistency in those areas. Heading is no different, but it has one bonus card that comes along with it. If you do it right, it won't hurt. If that's not motivation to read this section closely, then maybe you've already taken one too many off the top of the head.

As soon as you identify the flight of the ball, assess the point of its descent and move to the right, left, back, or forward to get into position. Much like an outfielder stands in a spot where she can catch a fly ball over her throw-ing shoulder, stand a few steps behind the spot where the ball will come down. Standing a couple steps behind the ball's landing area allows you to take a running start before heading the ball, thus improving the height of your jump. Track the ball through its entire flight. Don't look around to glance at other players. You should already know where they are. Maintain 100 percent focus on the ball.

Young players often assume that their neck provides the power when heading the ball. This is a misconception. Your neck provides a degree of force, but power is generated from your entire body. If you try to manufacture everything from your neck, chances are you'll miss your forehead. You'll more likely take it off the face or top of your head. Ouch! The power comes from your legs, torso, and upper body.

Arch Back and Snap Forward

Plant your feet slightly farther than shoulder-width apart and hold your arms out for balance and to hold off defenders. As the ball nears, arch your back, and lean back at the waist. Continue to watch the ball. Arching the back is a form of loading up. When kicking the ball, your leg swings back to load up before driving your foot through the ball. Arching your back is based on the same principle. It allows you to harness all your strength before exploding forward to the ball.

Once the ball enters striking distance, snap forward at the waist. Your entire upper body is still rigid, but your neck and head fire forward to strike the ball. Hit the ball with the spot just below your hairline (centered on your forehead). Keep your eyes open, your mouth shut, and drive straight through the ball. Head the ball, don't let the ball head you!

In most situations, strike the center of the ball. When heading the ball on goal off a cross, hit just above the center of the ball so it travels downward. Make contact with the ball at the top of your heading arc because that is the point where you generate the most power. In some cases, you'll want to head the ball over an opposing player or goalkeeper, so hit just below the ball's center point. Adjust the flight of your headballs by where you contact the ball, not where the ball hits your head.

Common Faults

When things go awry on a headball, it's frequently due to poor technique. Young kids tend to head the ball like they're a human pogo stick. They put their chin down and jump up. It's really cute, but won't produce favorable results.

The other major fault is closing the eyes. Think about taking a shot on goal, but closing your eyes the second before you kick the ball. You may kick the wrong part of the ball, which will diminish your degree of accuracy. You've got to watch the ball the entire way. Personally, if I'm going to use my head to strike something, I'm going to watch it as long as I can to make sure it hits the right part.

To avoid poor results (and a headache), keep your eyes open for as long as possible, and see the ball into your forehead.

Jumping for Headballs

To get to some headballs, you have to leave the ground. The ball may be out of your reach and you may be competing with an opponent to win the ball. Much like heading the ball with your feet on the ground, timing is critical when jumping up for a headball.

Jumping in the air to head the ball is two movements. First, jump up and arch back. Second, snap forward through the ball. You really use your entire body when jumping for headballs. You use your legs to provide the power to leap in the air. Your torso, abdominal muscles, and upper body are extremely important to fueling your snap forward to the ball. And of course, you use your head and neck to strike the ball.

Most players jump straight to the ball instead of jumping, arching, and then striking. Jumping straight to the ball can create a few

It's Fair to say . . .

In a match against Norway, I was told that my job was to win all the headballs in the midfield. That was to be my task to focus on entering the game. Norway fields a group of fairly tall women, so it was a challenging assignment.

I'm not tall, and my vertical leap is average but not great. The only way for me to carry out my assignment was to position myself to get a running start before jumping up for each headball opportunity. My vertical leap definitely improves when I jump off the run.

Each time I saw the ball go up in the air near the midfield, I'd immediately get to a spot a few yards behind the ball's landing area. As it descended, I ran forward and jumped up for the ball a split second earlier than my opponent. Not only did I elevate myself to maximum height by getting a running start, but my opponent would actually push me up a little higher as she jumped. Because I left the ground first, I'd win the headball. I won nearly every headball during that game.

Their coach was absolutely livid on the sidelines. He was yelling and screaming about how a 5' 3" player could win so many balls out of the air. I sort of took it as a compliment.

A great drill to improve your skills at jumping headers is to have a coach or teammate hold the ball above his head. Take a couple steps, jump up, and try to knock the ball out of his hands.

problems. For one, your headballs will be void of strength (no snap forward). Additionally, the ball may hit the top of your head, which will hurt. Also, you'll strike the bottom of the ball, causing the ball to go straight up instead of getting behind the ball and driving it downward. Elevate first, arch your back, and snap your forehead through the ball.

Timing entails constant practice. It takes time to train your body to synchronize the proper movements in midair. A great drill is to head the ball against a wall. It's something you can practice on your own to develop timing and proper technique.

Several factors dictate when to jump up for a headball. Obviously, the height of the ball and the speed it's traveling are important. But other elements such as the spin on the ball, the wind, the position to challenge for the headball (with regard to opponents), and the direction you want to head the ball influence your timing. Assess the surrounding factors as soon as you see the ball go up, and then time your jump accordingly.

Tisha Venturini doesn't have a high vertical jump on the national team. She ranks near the bottom of the team in that category, yet she wins almost every headball in her area. How? Her timing is exceptional and she wants to win the ball more than anyone who challenges her. Great timing and desire can overcome size and jumping ability.

Getting into Position

You can't expect to have the position of advantage for every headball. There will be many times when you'll be standing behind your mark. Defenders are notoriously whistled for a foul when jumping over the opposition. Here is how to win the ball without drawing a whistle.

Read the ball instead of watching the player. Maintain focus on playing the ball. Take a couple steps back so you can take a running start. As you jump, make sure all your energy is going straight up, not forward. If you allow your momentum to carry you forward, you're going to make obvious contact with the player in front of you and be called for a foul. Jump straight up and the ref will not whistle a foul . . . unless he or she is awarding a payback call.

Time your jump so you take off a split second before your opponent. You'll either get to the ball first by outjumping her, or you'll receive a helpful little push from her. When you're both jumping up for the ball, your opponent will actually jump into you because you've left the ground first. Make sense? When contact is made, she's the culprit (if a foul is called) because you had position.

Hold your arms out for balance, but keep them off your opponent's back. That's the easiest call for a ref to make.

Directing Headballs

Once you learn how to correctly head the ball, start working on directing your headballs to target areas. Heading can be used to pass, shoot, or clear a ball out to the side. I often use my head to pass the ball. If I were in transition play, for example, and the ball is up near my midsection, I'll head the ball to my teammate. Trapping the ball and controlling it at my feet takes too much time. Use the headball to keep the flow of play moving.

When directing headballs, open your body toward your target. Let the ball travel to you, and snap your head in the direction of your teammate. Although you're heading the ball to the side, still strike the ball with the middle of your forehead.

When flicking the ball on an angle, use the side of your head. The key to this skill is timing, which takes practice.

The key to directing headballs is the way you position yourself. Open your body in the direction of your target. Split the difference between where the ball is coming from and where you're heading it to. Say an aerial pass is coming from your left (point A) and you want to head the ball to the right (point B). Open your body to the ball so that your midsection faces the area in the middle of points A and B.

Concentrate on heading the left side of the ball (as it's traveling toward you). As the ball nears, snap your upper body and head from left to right. Strike the ball with your forehead, a touch to the right of center. Do not use the side of your head.

Flicks

Flicks are not a glamorized part of the game. You rarely hear someone say, "She's a great flicker." Despite it being a low-profile skill, flicks create dangerous situations on the offensive attack. They're used to set up goals off corner kicks, direct and indirect kicks, throw-ins, and crosses from the wing position. They can also set up breakaways off long kicks, goal kicks, and punts out of the backfield.

A flick is when you use the upper portion of your head to head the ball backwards. You sort of skim the ball with the top of your head so it caroms upward slightly and behind you. You can redirect the ball to the left or right behind you, but generally, you're altering the path of the ball a bit by bumping it up in the air.

As the ball approaches, extend your arms out for balance and keep your eyes open. Leap up as the ball is about to pass over your head. Tilt your head slightly upward and back as you contact the ball.

The ball should glance off the very top of your head. The less the ball touches your head, the less its path will be altered. If you catch too much of the ball, it will bounce high up and back. Your goal is to have the ball arc up slightly just to get over the defender's head.

Flicks are effective in the offensive end because play behind the potential flicker is unpredictable. Defenders can't anticipate the direction or distance of the flick. The ball may be flicked high and long, left or right, or it may not be flicked at all.

Flicking balls in the midfield off of goal kicks and punts is a little tougher. The ball is usually coming down, so it's probably going to hurt a little. But hey, that's why you've got to love playing the game.

Shooting

Heading the ball is one of the most reliable sources of scoring because it's such a quick, accurate form of shooting. As long as you're in position, track the ball, and strike it with your forehead, it's pretty hard to miss the net. On the run, you're like a human dart. The ball is your target and you just run through the ball with your head. Anytime the ball is above my waist near the goal, I use my head to shoot. It's quick, it's accurate, and you get some force behind the ball. The key is to head the ball down.

When you practice, work on heading balls that come from all different directions. Crosses off the dribble or restarts originate from varying locations, so it's important to become proficient at redirecting the ball on goal.

Accuracy is the key to heading crosses in front of the net. You can catch goalkeepers on the move or out of position in these situations, leaving them vulnerable to a well-placed shot. Headball goals are rarely scored because of their velocity but rather their location.

Boot Camp

I still have a little scar on my head from national team camp in the fall of 2001. We were scrimmaging in practice, and I went for a header and a player inadvertently booted me in the head.

I had a pretty decent-sized bump, but couldn't see if it was a bad cut. I was just sitting on the ground with my hand on my head. You know how when something doesn't look that good, your teammates are supposed to control their reaction so you don't freak out? Well, Millie and Tiff Roberts were not exactly stellar in that area. I took my hand off my head and they said, "Wooooaaaa! Oh my God!!"

I really appreciated that. I thought I was going to have some huge, nasty wound right in the middle of my forehead. But it was okay. I had a lump on my head for a few days, but that was nothing compared to what I initially thought I'd look like after soaking in the reaction of my good friends.

Diving Headers

Never be afraid to get your uniform dirty. When my jersey is painted with dirt and grass stains after a game, I feel like I put in a good day's work. Diving for a headball is a play that requires you to leave your feet and hit the turf.

On plays where you're racing to the ball and have to leave your feet to win it, I'd much rather use a diving header rather than sliding for the ball. When you slide feetfirst, what are you really going to do with the ball? Hit it with your cleats? By using your head, you can direct the ball to a teammate or on goal. It's a much more efficient method of approaching the play.

To execute a diving header, keep your head up and eyes on the ball. Dive straight out to the ball, rather than up toward the sky. Strike the ball with your forehead, and try to keep your eyes open as long as possible.

Drills

Progression Heading

In camps, we put kids through a heading progression drill to teach them proper technique. The goal is to make them understand that they should use their entire body to head the ball.

We start by having the kids lie on their stomachs and head the ball. It's all about using your neck and striking the ball with your forehead. Their ponytails fly over their foreheads and sometimes whack them in the face. From there they rise up to the sit-up position and add their upper body to snap through the ball, still keeping the neck movement from the previous exercise. They are down on both knees in the third stage and add arching their backs. Next, they stand up and incorporate their legs when heading the ball. Finally, we have them jump and work on their timing.

It's a great drill for beginners, because it teaches them to use everything from head to toe. The progression of exercises is the best way to learn the role of each body part.

On the Rebound

Proper form is important to heading the ball effectively, but timing is also an issue when you have to take to the air. This drill helps develop your timing when jumping up for headballs. All you need is a wall and your soccer ball.

Stand between six and ten yards away from the wall. Throw the ball up against the wall and as it rebounds, jump up to head the ball. You have to time your approach as well as your jump.

After you jump, arch back, snap forward, and head the ball down.

Vary your tosses to keep the exercise fresh and challenging. Toss balls higher or harder or to the right or left. Attempt to head each ball at the peak of your jump.

Jump Balls

This exercise simulates game play. It requires four players and a soccer ball.

To describe the drill, we'll label players A, B, C, and D. Player A has the ball and is the server. Approximately fifteen yards away, player B faces player A. Player C is standing right behind player B, and player D is standing approximately fifteen yards behind player C. Imagine the game monkey in the middle, only there are two players standing in the middle.

Player A serves the ball to player B. Player B's job is to flick the ball back to player D. Player C (the defender) is attempting to head the ball back toward player A. Gaining positioning and timing your jumps are critical in this drill. If player B succeeds in flicking the ball to player D, player D then becomes the server and players B and C switch roles. Player C is trying to flick to player A, and player B attempts to head the ball back to player D.

Continue running the exercise until all four players have assumed each role several times.

I love laying out for diving headers.

These photos depict a sequence of progression heading. Start by lying on your stomach with your head facing the server (1). Use just your neck to head the ball into the ground. Next, prop yourself up on your hands and feet, so you're facing the sky (2). Snap your upper body forward to head the ball (3). Notice that I use the middle of my forehead to strike the ball. Continue by standing up on your knees and thrusting forward to head the ball tossed by your partner (4). Use your forearms to break your fall (5). Now stand up and put one foot forward. Arch your back, and snap forward to head the toss (6–7). The last step is to stand with your feet aligned side by side (8). Keep your eyes on the ball as you arch back and snap your head forward to and through the ball.

"It's important that everyone on the field

works together with a common purpose."

Strategy

Enjoyment is the first step to playing the game of soccer. Without enjoyment, there is no purpose in playing the game. Once you've established that you like playing soccer and are interested in getting better, learning the fundamentals is the next step. After refining your technique and understanding when to use certain skills, repetitious training takes its turn at the wheel. The goal is not just to know how to perform specific crafts but to execute them instinctively. It's called muscle memory. If the game situation calls for me to bend an aerial pass from right to left, I've got to do so without running through a list of mechanical checkpoints in my head. As Nike puts it, you need to "just do it."

Upon completing all of these steps, you're ready for the battlefield. You possess the desire, the resolve, the fundamental skills, and the instinct. You've trained hard and have developed into the ultimate soccer player. You are now clearly the total package, right? Wrong. Sorry, you're almost there, but what you need now is a plan.

Individual soccer talent is a wonderful commodity, but to be successful and win champi-

onships, you've got to incorporate that talent into an overall strategy. Eleven players are on the field, and it's important that they all work together with a common purpose. Each player needs to know how their team is going to attack the opponent, how they plan to thwart the opposition's plan of attack, and what their individual role is to the team. In soccer, you've got to use your head for more than just headballs.

First-Grade Strategy

Things were much simpler when I was younger. If someone were to ask me what my offensive strategy was when I was eight years old, I would have opened my eyes really wide and said, "Get the ball, dribble, and score!" If the same person followed that question by asking me what my defensive strategy was, I would have responded, "Get the ball, dribble, and score!" Eventually, I learned that my approach (as authentic as it was) had a few holes in it. As I got older, I quickly learned that eleven

Understanding Formations

You may hear coaches talking about what type of formations they play and have difficulty interpreting the numbers. They speak in numbers like 4-3-3 and 4-4-2. Understanding what the numbers stand for is very simple.

Each number refers to a group of positions. There are three groups: defenders, midfielders, and forwards. The number references always start from the back and move forward. So if a coach mentions their team is playing a 4-3-3, it means there are 4 defensive backs, 3 midfielders, and 3 forwards. A 4-4-2 means there are 4 defensive backs, 4 midfielders, and 2 forwards. The goalkeeper is never mentioned. (Sorry, buddy.) Which formation a team should play is a decision based on their strengths and weaknesses, style of play, and the capabilities (or lack of) of the opposing team.

So now you know. The next time you're engrossed in a discussion that involves soccer strategy, you'll be able to follow along.

opposing players could stop one little runt from running around crazy with the ball. So I adapted. I passed the ball to Ronnie. Hey, if I can't have the ball, I might as well give it to a family member.

Seriously though, youth level teams are notorious for playing beehive soccer. What is beehive soccer? It's when everyone on the field swarms to the ball. The teams that end up winning games are the ones who figure out that by spreading their players around the field, many will go unmarked. Passing the ball to the players standing in open space will result in countless scoring chances. And that is soccer strategy in its most basic form.

Game strategy becomes a factor at higher levels of play. Formulating an effective game strategy is a matter of recognizing your strengths and weaknesses and considering the opposition's strengths and weaknesses. Teams need to identify what style of play best suits them when factoring in the capabilities of their roster. An intelligent game plan can make the difference between a win and a loss.

In this chapter, we'll first discuss offensive strategy and then talk about defensive strategy. Complementing your physical abilities with mental awareness can only benefit your player make-up. Your goal is to be the best possible player you can be. We've discussed the how and when of soccer, now it's time to talk about the why.

Offensive Strategy

Playing for so many different programs, I've been introduced to a lot of different offensive schemes. With some teams (like at UNC), we stuck to the same offensive plan every game. We forced the opposition to adjust to our style of play. On the national team, we are so versatile that we search for a profound weakness in the opponent and look to exploit it.

I'm going to summarize offensive plans used by the University of North Carolina, the U.S. national team, and the Philadelphia Charge. Each is unique, and they all required me to adjust my approach on the field.

Carolina Tar Heels: High-Pressure Soccer

A one-on-one mentality exists at UNC. The philosophy is that if we match up each of our players on the field with the respective opponent, we have the advantage. A lot of talented players are at UNC, which is supplemented by depth of talent. Passes are made in an effort to create a one-on-one situation for our players.

I could sum up Anson's strategy in two words: *high pressure*. We applied intense pressure up top with our forwards on their defenders. We tried to force the defensive opposition to make mistakes, get them to cough the ball up, and quickly counterattack. We played a 3-4-3 formation. We had 3 forwards play up front to maximize pressure on their defense coming out of the backfield and to create more options up front when we gained possession.

High pressure from attacking forwards only works if the midfielders and defensive line also move forward. If the forwards move up to pressure the defense and the midfielders sit back, the forwards will be easily beaten by a short pass into the space behind them. The same goes for the defensive backs. They have to move up as well and then everyone is marked up under high pressure.

The strategy implemented at Carolina relies on the cumulative efforts of everyone. All three forwards have to contribute as well as the backfield behind them. High-pressure soccer depends on one other major factor as well: fitness. You have to be incredibly fit to apply constant pressure without the ball. Most teams exert maximum effort when the ball is in their possession. At UNC, we exerted maximum effort for ninety minutes. In college, an unlimited substitution rule enables tired players to take a rest before going back in the game.

Playing three back. Playing a 3-4-3 formation means you only have three defensive backs. Ordinarily, the rule is to have more defenders than the opposing team has attackers. That way, extra defenders can cover for a teammate if she gets beat. Playing three back is a bit of a risk, but we always felt like our defenders were good enough to handle the opposing team's strikers.

To play three in the back, you must have three defenders who are skilled, fast, and practice good judgment. Moving forward out of the backfield requires communication and cooper-

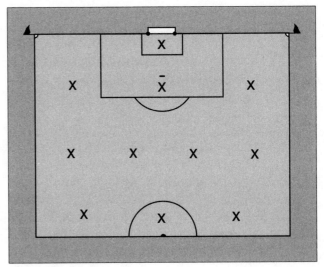

FIGURE 9.1
A 3-4-3 formation

ation. If you make a run forward, someone in the midfield needs to slide back to maintain the flat three in the back. Having only two defenders back is too risky.

U.S. National Team Strategy

The great thing about our national team is that we have such balance; we can play any formation and beat you. Lately, we've been working on a variety of different styles and will probably settle into a formation by the time the final roster is set for the 2003 World Cup. We used to play a 3-4-3 and then played a 4-3-3 in the 1999 World Cup. We played a 4-4-2 in the 2000 Olympics at Sydney, but there were times when we played a 4-3-3 and 3-4-3.

The matchup often dictates our formation and offensive strategy when competing internationally. As I said, we're extremely versatile and can be successful in a lot of different ways. So often, we'll look at the opponent's style of play, assess their weaknesses, and attack them.

For example, when playing a team like Norway, we need to have more defenders because their strategy is to kick it into the other team's defense and battle for the ball. It doesn't

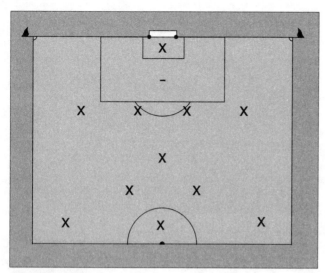

FIGURE 9.2
A 4-3-3 formation

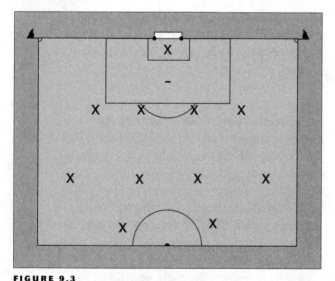

FIGURE 9.3
A 4-4-2 (flat back) formation

because they play a flat four in the back, which means they play four defenders in the backfield that stay in line no matter what. They never stagger, but rather move forward and back and side to side as a single unit. All the space is either behind the flat four or in front of it. The three forwards can pressure their four defenders so that Norway can't serve the ball long. Our success in beating their defense also relies upon the mobility of our forwards.

Because they never break the integrity of their defense, we usually play a lot of balls to our striker's feet as they check back to us. If Millie checks back to the midfield, the defender doesn't follow her. She stays in line with the other three defenders. So Millie will take the ball and turn.

The way to beat Norway is to take advantage of them when they overshift. They like to move everyone to the side of the field the ball is on and congest the playing area to strip the ball. Even their defensive players shift way over to the ball side. Usually, the defender playing the weak side will shift over only as far as the far post. Norwegian defenders move all the way over to the opposite post. They leave the weak side of the field wide open.

What we try to do is serve an entry ball to one side; make Norway collapse to one side; make a quick, one-touch pass out of that area; and then hit a one-touch pass across the field. We want to expand the field and catch them out of position. When they really overshift, we can almost hit a ball blindly to the opposite side of the field, and someone from our team will be there to collect it.

The trick is getting everyone coordinated and responding quickly. If you take more than one or two touches, they collapse on you so fast that you won't be able to hit that ball across the field. That's where the skill comes into play and complements your strategy.

So, on the U.S national team, we use a combination of speed, technical skill, and individual ability to play as a single, cohesive unit.

make sense to have numbers in the midfield because they just boot the ball long out of the back and over the midfield. It's an effective style of play for them and they are the only team in the world with a winning record against the United States.

So we put three players up front and play a 4-3-3. We like having three players up front

We search for that tiny leak in the opposing team's makeup and pound on it until the floodgates open.

The Philadelphia Charge Offensive Strategy

During the first season with the Philadelphia Charge, we played a 4-5-1, which is almost the exact opposite of what we played at UNC. When you hear of playing a 4-5-1, you usually think of a team that bunkers (sits everyone in the back). But we attacked quite well from that formation. It takes midfielders who possess offensive skills and who can run the field.

Our offensive strategy was to have our outside midfielders overlap and attack the defense. Because we had three center midfielders, we could also push two of them forward to bolster the offense. We'd keep one center midfielder back, which was usually me. My job was to cover the central area of the midfield that the two offensive mids just left.

The role of the lone forward is very important. Her job is to run to the side of the field that the ball was being brought up and then check to the ball. When she receives a pass, she holds onto the ball. This buys time so the midfielders can get forward. Most of our runs are from behind the ball and then moving forward.

Although you may think the most integral skills a forward should possess are dribbling and shooting, that's not the case in a 4-5-1. She has to have great receiving skills, the ability to hold the ball while fending off opponents, and, finally, good passing ability. The forward in a 4-5-1 constantly distributes the ball back to the supporting midfielders as well as the overlapping runners. Mandy Clemens plays forward on the Charge and is great at holding onto the ball and making smart decisions. Kelly Smith is another great forward with different strengths. If she can get turned with the ball to face up to her defender, I'd tell her to go to goal. She's an

No Luck for the Irish

During my freshman year at UNC, we played Notre Dame in the national championship game. Notre Dame had eliminated us the year before in the semifinal game, so emotions were riding high entering the game.

The Irish played a 3-4-3 like we did, and with our strikers, we knew it would be extremely dangerous to play us that way. Everyone in the country knew we played three forwards up front and usually adjusted accordingly. The Irish refused to adjust their formation.

By halftime, the ND coach switched his formation. We were so dominant up front, they had to do something to keep our forwards under control. We won the game 1–0 in overtime and regained our national championship status. It was my first NCAA title and was a feeling that I will never forget.

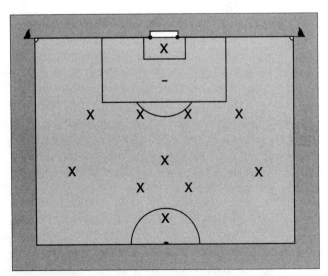

FIGURE 9.4
A 4-5-1 formation

The Great Offensive Players

A lot of players have great offensive skills, but then there are those who are great offensive players. They always seem to create situations that present danger to the defense. There's no question that speed, dribbling moves, passing ability, and finishing are offensive skills that contribute heavily to an offensive player's prowess on the field. But the great offensive players possess those intangibles that separate them from the pack.

One of the traits that they carry is vision. They know where everyone is at any given time. And I'm not just talking about their teammates but opponents as well. If you know where everyone is at all times then you'll be aware of the weakness in the defense that you can exploit. Great offensive players are also very deceptive. A player who combines skill with deception is very difficult to mark.

I've played with a handful of individuals who possess individual skills that are so good it makes them special offensive players. Kelly Smith plays like she has Velcro on her shoes. The ball just sticks to her feet. She has a fair amount of speed, but she's also strong, very agile, and has incredible foot skills. She's a great attacking player.

Millie is tough because she is so quick. If you stop paying attention to her for a split second, she's gone. For someone as fast as she is, she dribbles through tight spaces extremely well. Usually people who are extraordinarily fast possess mediocre foot skills. They rely on their speed and don't have to develop great touch. With Millie, that is not the case and it's probably why she's the best offensive player in the world right now. Her one-on-one skills are unparalleled.

incredible dribbler and strong enough to hold off multiple defenders.

By playing the 4-5-1, we pass a lot of balls to feet and depend heavily on the support system. The player holding the ball has to have multiple options. With only one player up top, it's not as if you can dump balls into the corner, because you'll lose possession every time. You've got to play the ball to feet and have a lot of off-the-ball movement.

In the clubhouse before a national team match. It's important that each player understands the overall game strategy.

It's Fair to say . . .

Teams have all types of strengths and weaknesses. Some have speed, others have size or even great technical skill. The best teams have a combination of strengths and few weaknesses. If you have all three, I would sure hate to meet up with you in competition. But here's a brief description of how I'd manage a team that possesses a high degree of one of these three strengths.

Team Based on Speed

I'd put three forwards up front and make sure I had players in the back who could kick the ball. If you don't have the skill to maintain possession, go with your strength and use your speed. Speed is not something you can teach, and it makes things difficult for opposing players who don't have it. I'd have one skilled player in the midfield who is able to handle the ball and distribute. I'd have defensive and midfield players bang the ball into space and let the forwards fly. It may not be the prettiest soccer in the world, but you've got to go with what you've got.

Team Based on Physical Size

Honestly, I'd play to get free kicks and restarts. I'd try to create the most possible situations where the ball is sent into the box in front of the goal. Have offensive players hit balls off defenders to force corner kicks and long throw-ins. If you have superior size in the box, the defenders are helpless and now it's something the goalkeeper has to deal with.

Team Based on Skill

I'd play a possession game. I'd go with a 4-3-3. I like having three forwards up top because it gives you so many options. With technical skill you can vary your plan of attack. You can tire a team out with precision passing and combination play. You can be unpredictable with your attack, which is exactly what you want. The defense will never be able to anticipate.

Cindy Parlow combines quickness, size, and skill. For being 5' 10", she's extremely agile and great with the ball at her feet. She's a very tough player to mark.

Michelle Akers was great for so many reasons, but the one thing I'll always remember about her is that her first touch always had a purpose. She never trapped the ball. She was always going somewhere with it. She knew where the space was before receiving the ball and immediately took it into that space. Her first touch would be to avoid pressure or to beat a player and, with her size and strength, she would rarely lose possession. She'd receive the ball while exploding into space and immediately put herself into a dangerous position.

Defensive Strategy

Soccer is a game of situations and, because of that, there are so few certainties. But I can make you a guarantee in one area. If you don't let the other team score, you can't lose. I know, tell that to the women's Chinese national team right? They didn't allow us to score in the 1999 World Cup final and we won the title, but that was an extraordinary situation. Most games are not decided by a shootout. Keep the opponent off the scoreboard and your team is going places.

Defensive players rarely grab headlines. It's not a glamour position. But if you play great defense as a unit, people will start to take notice. The great defenders take pride in their play. Pride allows you to play with passion on the field. It motivates you to play with a sense of focus and direction and it develops a cohesive attitude among your teammates. A proud defense is difficult to penetrate.

When we won the U-16 national championship on the Sunnyvale Roadrunners, our defense had tremendous pride. In the backfield, we called ourselves the "No-Goal Patrol." We didn't have any set strategy. We just swarmed the ball and absolutely suffocated the attacking offense. We gave them no chance to execute.

During our run through the state, regional, and national tournaments, we gave up just one goal. One goal in more than three months of games! The goal came in the first round of State Cup. We were winning 8–0 and our coach decided to let the defensive backs play forward and the forwards play defense. That's the only time anyone put a ball in our net.

Our defense played with such intensity that we got to a point where we stopped trying to shut out teams. We set our sights higher. We focused on not allowing any *shots* during a game. By giving up no goals, you're pretty much guaranteed of a win. But to give up no shots? Our goalkeeper must have been bored out of her mind.

Team Defense

Playing great defense is a commitment made by the entire team. The defensive backfield provides leadership, but the team can only achieve perfection if the midfielders and forwards contribute to the overall defensive cause. Offensive goals garners ink in the newspaper, but great defense will generate Ws in the standings.

The defensive strategies for Carolina, the U.S. national team, and Philly have varied somewhat because we play different formations. The primary objective of each, however, is one and the same. First and foremost, deny the ball.

Mark your player tightly and don't allow her to get the ball. If each player accomplishes that, nobody will beat you.

This is much easier said than done. Dynamic offensive players, countering offensive schemes, transition play, and restarts all present opposing teams opportunities to possess and move the ball around. But always keep your primary objective in mind. Try to deny your mark from receiving the ball. It's an aggressive form of defense.

Taking the action to the offense. At Carolina, our defensive mindset was identical to our offensive plan. We applied high pressure all over the field. We would deny the ball, double team, tackle aggressively, and concentrate on defending every inch of the field. Every player has a responsibility to cover a certain territory and tackle everything in it (dominate). If each player expands that territory by width and depth, then the territory will start to overlap. The opponent will feel as if fourteen players are on the field defending them.

The national team starts off game with high pressure in opponents' defensive third and then adjusts where we start our pressure. With the skill of teams like China, Brazil, and Germany, you can't apply high pressure for too long because you'll tire quickly. We maintain pressure, but back off and start pressuring a little farther back on the field. To pressure all over the field for ninety minutes is a long time against teams who have technical skill, especially because we're only allowed three substitutions per game.

With Philly, we have the one forward playing up front (4-5-1). Her job is to force the defense to one side of the field as they come out of the backfield. She's not expected to win the ball, just get the flow of players going to one side or the other. Our midfielders then shove up into spaces and clog up the passing lanes. We try to trap them on that side and then intensify our pressure.

When the dribbler heads toward the sideline, this presents a golden opportunity to double up and trap her.

It's very important that you understand your individual role within the defensive strategy, but you've also got to learn everyone else's responsibilities as well. At Carolina, by the time you were a senior, you could recite everywhere you were supposed to be in any situation and also where everyone else was supposed to be. When it comes down to crunch time, a player may find herself out of position or forget her responsibility. You've got to tell her where to be and what she's supposed to be doing. Good defense depends on everyone doing her job. Eleven focused individuals play as one cohesive unit.

Defensive Priority List

1. Deny the ball.

2. Challenge the pass.

3. Don't let her turn.

4. Don't let her penetrate.

5. Slow her down until support comes.

Diffusing the Offensive Rush

Most offensive attacks are born of transition, but many start out of the defensive backfield.

It's similar to a basketball game. The point guard dribbles the ball up the floor while her teammates get into position. How easily you want to allow the point guard to bring the ball up the floor is a matter of strategy. Do you want to run a full-court press, half-court press, or let her dribble the ball up the floor uncontested? If Anson Dorrance were a basketball coach, I'd bet the ranch on what his answer would be to that question. He'd play a full-court press from tip-off to the final buzzer.

While each player on the field should be able to play individual defense (covered later in this chapter), there are additional responsibilities specific to your position on the field. Forwards have a different agenda than the defensive backs, and the midfielders, well, they just have to run all over the place. Playing defense entails more than marking up and tackling. It requires you to perform within the structure of your defensive responsibilities.

Forwards. When playing on the front line, always keep this in mind: you are a soccer player first and a position player second. Soccer players can play both offense and defense. Mia, Cindy Parlow, and Kelly Smith are all examples of prolific scorers who play defense. They don't

By anticipating the pass, you can get a quick jump on your mark and intercept the ball.

stop playing when possession is lost. They know they're most dangerous when they have the ball at their feet, so it serves them well to do everything in their power to get the ball from their competitors.

The biggest responsibility of forwards is to make play predictable for their teammates behind them. When the ball is coming out of the backfield, apply pressure to the backs, and force the opponent to one side of the field. If she makes a mistake, you're there to capitalize with a quick counterattack. If not, you're making it easier for the next line of defense to read the next pass.

At times, we try to force the ball into the middle of the field. Communication is essential so that we're all on the same page. If the forwards are forcing the ball into the middle and the midfield is anticipating play to move to the sidelines, it creates a problem. Game strategy works when it's a team effort.

Forwards can take the biggest risks because they have two lines of defense behind them before the goalkeeper. They can be aggressive in trying to strip the ball from the dribbler. If you have a chance at the ball, go in hard. Even if you don't come away with it, you may force a bad pass. Every effort is worth its weight in gold.

Midfielders. You'd better be in good shape when you're playing midfield. Without question, the midfielders run the most throughout a game. They're the team support staff. They support the forwards on offense and the backfield on defense. Games are often won and lost in the midfield and their impact on a game is monumental. It's a great position to play because you see a lot of action and are involved in every aspect of the game. I love it. You just better get your butt in shape, because you have to run a lot for a long period of time.

When playing defense in the midfield, your job is to condense and shut down that space in front of you and behind the forwards. Look to intercept errant passes or anticipate the direction of the pass out of the back. If the opponent is fortunate enough to advance the ball to past your forwards, stop her right there. When I play midfield, I try to double up on players in every direction. I try to tackle everything that comes in my area, but I'll also try to double up from side to side to force mistakes.

Midfielders have a similar mentality to the forwards when it comes to pressuring, but you have to be a little more conservative. Taking too many risks can be costly and allow the opposition to get behind you. This forces a defensive teammate from the back to move up and pressure the ball. Consequently, your last line of defense loses strength. Make sure your risks in the midfield are educated risks.

Defenders. As the opponent moves the ball into your defensive third of the field, she's getting closer and closer to goal. You want to get the ball back in your team's possession, but you also have to think about defending your goal. Keep your eyes on the ball, but make sure you're marking tight. This is not the time to break for the ball with reckless abandon.

Communication is a huge responsibility of the defensive players. Their job is to instruct the teammates in front of them. If I'm part of a backfield, we'll tell the forwards and midfielders, "force left," "force outside," or "force to me." Give your teammates direction so you can work together to slow down and then stifle their attack. With your midfielders' backs to you, the only way to stay on the same page is to use your vocal chords. As the ball gets into your defensive third, the goalkeeper (who is constantly giving direction) takes over to conduct and orchestrate.

When the opponent breaks through your midfield, do your best to slow things down. Push the attack to one side if possible, and simply contain them. Slow or delay the dribble to give your midfielders time to recover. Denying the ball, forcing the attacker to pass the ball back where it came from, or not allowing her to turn and face the goal are all methods of slowing play down. Take away or reduce the momentum of their attack and your teammates in the midfield and up front will quickly regroup and strengthen your line of defense.

Individual Defense

Playing good defense is about attitude. It's a decision that you make with yourself. You make an internal commitment to go all out and do everything in your power to defend. You have to be tough. You have to have grit. When you get knocked down, you get up immediately. Never let your mark think she got the best of you. Get right back up in her face, and let her know that she's got to deal with you for ninety minutes. I want my attacker to know that every time she tries to get the ball, I'm going to be right there to make her life miserable.

In every game, I try to make a statement with the first tackle I make. I want to let the player know that nothing is going to be easy from the first to the ninetieth minute. I'm going to be breathing down her neck with such agitation that she'll absolutely hate me by halftime.

Playing defensive sounds pretty fun, huh? Or should I say borderline insane?

Obviously, physical skills have a major role in defensive play, but the mental aspect is absolutely crucial. I know a lot of players who possessed exceptional soccer skills but were only average defenders because they didn't set their mind to it. You've got to focus on defending. Once you do that, you're on your way to shutting down opponents.

I should mention one other thing. You know that human emotion called *fear*? Well, it has no place in the defensive backfield. So if you want to be a good defender, find your mark and lose the fear.

You can't be afraid of getting hurt. You put your body in some pretty vulnerable positions,

Push the dribbler toward the sideline to contain her. This limits her attacking options and slows down the offensive rush.

but playing timidly will only make you more vulnerable. Understand that you're going to sustain some bumps and bruises. For example, when you're trying to win a headball, the offensive player is trying to flick the ball one way, and you're trying to head it in the opposite direction. To win those balls, you have to get above her head, so inevitably you're going to take some balls off your chest, neck, and face. That's simply the reality of being a good defender. Accept the fact that you're going to take some balls between the eyes because it comes with the territory. Now we can move on.

Defending the Dribbler

When you're defending the player with the ball, always consider the situation and your surroundings. Is she boxed in a corner? Is a lot of space open behind you? Are you the last line of defense? Is she extremely fast? Is she trying to get off a shot? Is she only a threat with her right foot? All of these things factor into your approach. You may want to just contain the dribbler, slow her down, force her to one side, or try to strip her of the ball. Whatever the case may be, understand the situation so you can practice good judgment.

When I'm defending the dribbler, I look at the ball. First of all, that's what I'm after. I don't care where the player is going, I just want what's at her feet. She can step over, around, and behind the ball until she's blue in the face. The ball is still sitting in the same spot.

Second, if she takes a touch that's too long, it presents an opportunity to win the ball. If I'm busy focusing on the player's hips or eyes, I won't see that the ball is too far from her foot and that I can poke it away. A lot of coaches stress looking at the belt buckle (or hips). I'm not a big proponent of that approach; it's probably adapted from the way American football coaches teach tackling.

You need to have an idea of what the rest of her body is doing; a sense of awareness. It can help you anticipate. Let's say, for example, a fair amount of space is behind you. The dribbler may try to push the ball past you to one side and run around the opposite side. If you're just looking at the ball, you'll have no indication to which side she's planning to run past you. By the time she's kicked the ball, it's too late to cut her off to the opposite side. She'll be by you, off and running before you know what happened.

When the opportunity presents itself, take a stab at poking the ball away from the dribbler.

When I win a ball, I look to the teammate who is farthest up the field first. I'm trying to put as many people out of the game as possible with my pass. If everyone is marked up top, I look for a shorter pass. It's kind of like a quarterback making a check across the field. You have options 1, 2, 3, and 4. Option 1 is probably going to gain the most yards, but if it's covered by the defense, you opt for a shorter, safer pass. Someone is always open within one or two touches.

If you opt for a short pass, try not to pass it square (directly east to west). Angled passes are much safer because they are difficult to intercept.

Take a stab at it. Patience is key to stripping the ball from the dribbler. You have to wait for the right moment. Don't just dive in at any time. Wait until she touches a ball that strays too far from her foot. Once you pick your moment, take stab at the ball. Don't take a huge swing to attack the ball. It takes too long, and the dribbler will see it coming. Use a short, compact jab at the ball to surprise the dribbler. Think of a snake waiting to attack its prey. It sits perched almost motionless and, without warning, snaps its head forward in an instant. Spontaneity is a useful weapon.

Playing the Ball Out of the Backfield

When you win the ball in your backfield, the opponent's mindset immediately changes. Attacking forwards think about getting the ball back. Midfielders begin to retreat in defense of the inevitable transition. Defenders find their marks and get goal-side.

Your team quickly adjusts their train of thought from defensive to offensive. Attacking players look for open space, midfielders move to support the backfield, and defenders look for a smart pass.

Dribbling Out of the Backfield

There are few times when you should dribble the ball out of the backfield. Don't make a habit of it, because you'll get yelled at all the time. Trust me, I'm speaking from experience. When I first got to UNC, Anson probably had a chronic sore throat from yelling at me. My natural instinct was to dribble my way out of trouble and create. Let's just say I had to learn to calm and control my instinctual decision making.

When I win the ball out of the backfield, I look to the farthest teammate upfield first.

If your teammates are marked up in front of you and there is space up ahead, keep the ball at your feet and take off. Force a defender to leave her mark and play you. That creates a two-on-one passing option. Instead of trying to force a pass to a player covered and risk losing the ball, dribble the ball and wait for something to open up.

Pay attention to your surroundings before taking off with the dribble out of the backfield. If there is a lot of traffic and the dribbling is tight, it's best to get rid of the ball. Send it upfield or to a teammate on the outside. Taking too many touches in tight areas is a situation where you can get stripped and become victim of a quick counter attack.

Slide Tackling

Slide tackling is a defensive tactic used as a last resort. I try not to leave my feet if I can avoid it because you're out of the play that follows.

Generally, I slide tackle a player when I'm beat. If my mark gets behind me with the ball and is going to the goal, I'll slide in out of desperation to knock the ball from her possession. Make sure you go directly for the ball. If your feet get tangled up in her legs, the ref may blow the whistle, or even worse, flash a card.

Depending on where the ball is, either poke the ball with your toe point, or if you're coming from the side hook your foot around the ball to gain possession. With the player dribbling forward, she'll probably fall over the ball if you hook it right. Get up and take control of the ball.

Extend your sliding leg out as far as possible and bend your other leg at the knee and tuck it behind or underneath you. Think of a baseball slide. Try to keep your arms in the air to avoid jamming your wrist into the ground as you slide.

I've learned to slide with either leg, so I slide with whichever leg is in stride. It's an advantage that allows me to reach some balls quicker. I suggest that you try to learn to slide tackle with either leg.

Situational Defense

Throughout a game, many factors may force you to adapt your defensive approach. A player's strengths (speed or size), player advantages, and the scoreboard can affect the way you go about your business. Here are my suggestions of how to respond to game situations.

Marking a player who is faster than you. When I play a faster player, I mark her a lot tighter when she doesn't have the ball. The best way to shut down a player with speed is to deny her the ball. So I'm right on her everywhere she goes. If the player is able to receive a pass, I stay tight on her and don't let her turn. By keeping her back to the goal, I take away her speed.

There will be times during the game when your mark will have the ball facing you. If she's got momentum coming at you, give her some space. Back off and try to contain her. As soon as you detect which direction she's going to try to run by you, start running a little earlier than her to maintain a cushion.

Chasing fast players is tough. If they're fast and smart, they'll cut you off once they get behind you. In this situation, keep in mind where the goal is. Take an angle that will put you between the player and the goal. There's no reason for you to simply chase her from behind because you may never catch up.

Marking a player who is bigger than you. You might say I've had a little experience in this category. To be honest, I enjoy marking big players. I love the challenge and really try to wear them down mentally.

Winning balls out of the air is difficult. You can do one of two things: leave the ground early and try to get to the ball first, or try to deflect their flick or headball. The latter may yield a few shots to the face, but like I said, that comes with the territory of playing good defense.

When a bigger player is holding the ball, she's going to try to use her size against you. To combat her size, get really low. If you remain upright, she'll easily shove you around and have her way with you. The lower your center of gravity is, the harder it is for you to get pushed around.

Remain patient and either wait for her to make a mistake with her touch or for one of your teammates to come over and double up on her. Don't move in too close too fast. If she gets a hold of you, she'll just use her weight and leverage to knock you away from the ball. Battle her size with quickness and smarts.

Two on one. When you're in a two-on-one situation and you're the one, make it a one on one. Take a bending approach to the dribbler so you put yourself in or near the passing lane to her teammate. Don't anticipate the pass because if the dribbler keeps the ball, she'll go right past you. Always remember the player with the ball in this situation is the most dangerous player.

Philadelphia Charge head coach Mark Krikorian has a last-minute discussion with Heather Mitts before a WUSA match.

The key to defending this play is timing. If you sit in the passing lane too long, the dribbler will take off. If you leave prematurely, the dribbler will easily beat you with a pass to her teammate. Stay in the lane long enough to force the dribbler to keep the ball and then use some aggression to attack and contain the dribbler.

Playing defense with a one-goal lead. Play the same defense, but don't attack as much when your mark has the ball at her feet. I actually mark tighter to deny the ball. A player can't operate or create without the ball. And as I said earlier, if she does receive a pass, don't let her turn.

I know that young players often give more cushion when protecting a lead, because they're afraid of getting beat by marking too tightly. You're really asking for trouble if you give too much cushion. It gives the player room to make things happen.

If you're marking a player who is bigger than you, lower your center of gravity to avoid getting pushed around.

"Restarts can spark hope, and ultimately victory,
for a team that is being dominated on the field."

Restarts

The team that wins the soccer game is usually the one who controls the flow of play. This isn't an exact science, but more often than not, final scores reflect which team dominated play on the field. The wildcard, however, is restarts.

Restarts, more than any other aspect of soccer, have the ability to balance out the playing field. They present golden opportunities for goals. Restarts can spark hope, and ultimately victory, for a team that is being dominated on the field.

A restart is a play that continues competition after the game has been stopped. A whistle is blown by the referee, and play ceases. Possession of the ball is awarded to one of the teams that will restart play. Corner kicks, free kicks, throw-ins, and goal kicks are all examples of restarts. They are distinct from the standard flow of the game in that they are a closed skill. By *closed skill*, I mean a situation in which the offensive team (the team who is awarded possession) is in complete control of what transpires on the field. Play is stopped, and the ball is restarted from a specific area on the field. The

team in possession can set up their players in precise positions and run a play much like you would in football or basketball.

All other play is considered an open skill. Your actions are largely based on reaction. Plays can be run, but on a smaller scale, such as give-and-go or an overlapping run. These plays are accomplished by becoming familiar with your teammates and their tendencies and being cognizant of your surroundings. But because play is continuous, there isn't an opportunity to arrange players in position and initiate play on cue.

Restarts are a closed skill and represent a component of the game that is completely separate from regulation play. They can bear enormous impact on the match's outcome.

Norway is a team that plays for restarts. They're exceptional at corner kicks and knock balls off our defenders just to gain a corner kick. They have very big players that are difficult to defend when the ball is in the air, so restarts play to their strengths. Restarts play a vital role in Norway's success.

It's Fair to say . . .

One of my most painful losses during my career was engineered by a restart. In my junior year at UNC, we were vying for our third consecutive national title. We were 25–0 going into the championship game against the University of Florida and were a game away from completing a perfect season.

Just 5:23 into the match, the Gators were awarded a direct kick. Danielle Fotopoulos stepped up and blasted a left-footed shot over our wall that hit the crossbar and dropped into the left side of the net. It was a perfect strike and they had a 1–0 lead.

For the rest of the game, we pounded away at Florida with shots, and they pounded away at us with fouls. We outshot the Gators 21–6 and they outfouled us 31–4. That fantastic goal by Danielle held up, and Florida won the national championship 1–0.

Although we dominated play in that game, Florida capitalized on a restart opportunity. It was a tough loss to swallow, but they played a great game. And that loss made me more deter- mined than ever to win the national crown my senior year.

With restarts, play is stopped which allows the offense to set up and run a play.

players and make sure that no one deemed dangerous is left unattended.

On the opposite end, the offense is allowed to implement a play by design. Dictated by the type of restart and its location, set plays are installed to confuse defenses and create scoring chances. Much like a quarterback calls a play in the huddle, or a point guard calls out a play dribbling the basketball upcourt, restart plays are meticulously planned. Each offensive player in the play has a specific role. If each player car- ries out their individual assignment and the play is executed as designed, an opportunity to score is imminent.

A Set Defense Versus an Organized Attack

Because restarts are executed from a stoppage of play, they wear a different face in comparison to regulation play. Play is stopped, and the defense has time to stockpile defenders in the backfield. On free kicks, they even set up a wall in front of the shooter to block a portion of the goal. Defensive players mark up with offensive

Organization and Discipline

Organization and discipline are the keys to properly executing and producing off of restarts. Each player must know what she's sup- posed to do, why she's doing it, and what her teammates are supposed to do. Let me give you an example of why it's important to know the role of each teammate.

Let's say the restart is a corner kick, and your job is to start at the far post and run across the goalmouth as the ball is struck. You're supposed to beat the goalkeeper to the ball. On the corner, the ball is hit low. You're about a half a step in front of the goalie, who is coming out aggressively to beat you to the ball. Instead of trying to make a difficult shot on the run, you use your body to block the keeper and allow the ball to run across the goal. You can do this because you know you have another teammate running to the far post and a second teammate behind her just in case the ball squeezes through. By knowing they are there, you can let the ball go and allow them to easily touch the ball into an open net.

And that scenario also indicates why discipline is so significant. Your teammates are counting on you to be in your predetermined spot. You've got to make your run regardless of how insignificant it may seem. Even if the ball is nowhere near you, continue with your run. The moment you're not where you're supposed to be is the moment the ball ends up in that spot. It's inevitable. Maintain strong discipline so that your team has all its bases covered.

Offensive Restarts

Because restarts can have such an impact on games, it's essential that you understand them from both an offensive and defensive mindset. When you hear the term *restart*, you typically think of offensive plays, so we'll discuss the offensive viewpoint first.

Throw-Ins

The most basic of all the restarts is the throw-in, and because it's so basic, it's often not given proper attention by players. I've been called for foul throws at Carolina and with the national team, and I can't even describe how stupid I felt. It's a dumb mistake that results in a loss of possession.

A throw-in is awarded when the opposing team last touches or plays the ball before the entire ball passes beyond the sideline (touchline). The ball can be thrown in any direction from the point where it crosses the sideline. Make sure both feet are on the ground and behind the line. You can stand flat-footed, walk up, or take a running start to initiate a throw-in.

Squaring your shoulders to the target decreases the risk of a foul throw. Remember, straight back and straight forward with both hands.

With two hands, bring the ball straight back over your head, continue until the ball is completely behind your head, and deliver the ball straight over your head (forward). This is done in one continuous motion. Use both hands with equal force. If you try to use more force with one arm, a foul throw will be called. Also, throw the ball so your teammate can collect it easily, not so it bounces up into her body. Make your teammates look good.

In my mind, it's most important to maintain possession when throwing the ball in. There is no rule that states you have to throw the ball forward. If a teammate is open upfield, that's great, but don't force the ball into a player who is tightly marked. Survey the area and look for a teammate who is open to receive the ball.

Good teams will mark tightly, so there may not be any teammates open. Be patient. There is no time clock that forces you to rush your throw. Give your teammates time to break loose and make a run. After throwing the ball, hop back onto the field of play and give your teammate the option for a backpass. She might be under pressure.

You might also help your teammates get open by pump-faking a throw. Quarterbacks and basketball players use pump-fakes all the time to throw off defenses. Faking a throw can coax a defender into leaning in one direction, allowing your teammates to break free in the opposite direction. Just make sure that your body is square to your ultimate target. If you throw across your body, the ref will whistle a foul throw.

Some players can throw the ball from the touchline all the way to the goalmouth. On the Philadelphia Charge, Jan Tietjen and Erica Iverson have long throw-ins. It is a great weapon to have on your team. Any time the ball is knocked over the sideline down in the attacking third, it's like having a corner kick from the sideline.

Much like a corner kick, organize your runs so each player has a defined role. There are many ways of executing long throw-ins (and corner kicks), but there are a few that I like. Have a player running to the ball for a flick and runners moving into the six-yard box. There should also be one or two players stationed at the top of the box.

Even if your team doesn't have a player who can reach the goal, throw-ins in the offensive third can still present offensive scoring threats. Have a player make a run from the goal toward the thrower, and flick the ball back toward the goal. The precise direction of flicks is difficult to anticipate, so it creates a dangerous situation in front of the goal for the defense. During practice, learn the maximum distance your teammate can throw the ball, and run directly to that spot. By practicing your runs, you'll develop a sense of timing with your teammate throwing, so you and the ball arrive at the spot simultaneously.

Corner Kicks

One aspect of soccer that remains constant regardless of the level of play, corner kicks create excellent scoring chances. Offensive players can't be called offsides on corner kicks, so it allows attackers to aggressively make their runs and position themselves wherever they want.

Each player on offensive has a job, so it's important to be disciplined. Time your run so that you'll get to your spot as the ball arrives. That means if you're making a near-post run, you've got to get in gear immediately. A ball hit to the near post takes very little time to get there, so you've got to start early and streak to the spot. Conversely, you may want to delay your run a bit when making a far post run. It's a longer distance for the ball to travel to reach the far post.

Striking corner kicks. At the youth levels of soccer, the goal is to simply put the ball in front of the net when striking a corner kick. As we progress to more advanced levels of play, corner kicks are hit with a purpose.

I raise my hand and drop it before each corner kick. This signals the offense to start their runs.

When taking a corner kick, drive through the ball instead of sending in a floater. It will give the defense less time to react.

Several thoughts run through my head before I approach a corner kick for the Philadelphia Charge. Is the goalkeeper weak in the air? Is she aggressive coming forward to balls but timid going back? Where are the strong headers on my team? What areas were open on the last corner? Where did I hit my last corner? Why is my Uncle Bob trying to start another wave in the stands?

If a keeper is really aggressive coming out of the goal, I might try to stretch her out. I'll hit an out swinger and bend the ball away from the goal. The keeper may think she can get to the ball as it leaves my foot and vacate the goalmouth, but eventually realize she's in no-man's-land. By then, it will be too late for her to recover. Another option is to hit a low ball to the near post, especially if I noticed it wasn't covered on a previous kick. Conversely, I'll drive the ball to the far post if the goalie is reluctant to go back on a ball. In essence, each time I take a corner kick, I approach it with a purpose.

The "where" of my kicks fluctuates with each corner, however, the "how" remains consistent. Wherever I send the ball, it's driven. I never send a floater. It gives defenders and, more importantly, the goalkeeper more time to assess, adjust to, and play the ball.

Driven balls allow less time for defenders to react. Remember, the offensive team holds an advantage because only the attackers know where they're running. Why slow things down for the defense? Hit the ball hard. Attackers will need to only redirect the ball to finish because the pace is already there.

Free Kicks

Direct and indirect kicks are awarded when the opponent commits a foul. Understand which type of kick is awarded before running a play. On direct kicks, the shooter can score off of a direct shot on goal. No one else has to touch the ball. On indirect kicks, another player has to touch the ball before it goes in the net for the goal to count. It can be a player on either team (including the goalie), but it has to contact another player to register a goal.

On offense, the idea is to get the keeper to take a step or commit to one direction and shoot toward the opposite direction. Deception and confusion disrupt the goalie's ability to set and anticipate the timing and direction of the shot. Players running over the ball, faking a shot, faking a pass, or rolling the ball back to a teammate can accomplish this. Keep the goalie guessing so she can't set.

Running plays. There are countless plays to run off of free kicks. What you run depends on the placement of the ball, the goalkeeper's strengths and/or weaknesses, how the defense is set up, and whether you've got a sharp shooter on your team. If Michelle Akers is wearing your team's uniform, just let her rip it.

Lately we've been trying an assortment of plays on the national team. We have one where Julie Foudy stands in the wall. Three players stand behind the ball: one right behind it, one to the left, and one to the right. If the ball is on the left side of the field, Julie stands a little left of center in the wall. The offensive player lined up to shoot runs up to the ball to shoot and touches a firm push pass to Julie in the wall. Julie one-times a pass out to the player on the right (just outside the wall) and she fires a shot. The goalkeeper's vision is blocked by the wall during the two touch passes, giving her minimal time to shift over and cut off the angle to a shot coming from the right side.

There are several basic plays shown in the diagrams, but always keep a few things in mind.

- Before running the play, look for any teammates who are blatantly left open in a dangerous scoring position. The defense and goalkeeper become so concerned setting up a wall that they may forget to pay attention to the attackers. If a player is standing by herself in a position to score, abort the play and send her a pass immediately.

- Do your best to sell the play. The object of players running over the ball or faking shots is to deceive the goalie. To get her to move, you've got to convince her that your actions are genuine. So if you're supposed to fake a shot and step over the ball, approach the ball like you're really going to shoot it. Don't just run through the motions. The only way to get the keeper to bite is to appear as if she thinks you're about to shoot.

The first player runs over the ball in an attempt to get the goalkeeper to commit. Whether your job is to fake a strike, pass, or shoot, always execute your runs with intensity to sell the play.

- Continue your run as the player shoots. Do not stop and become a spectator. If your job is to run over the ball and then run off the wall, keep running and frame the goal on the shot. You should always have someone running to the near and far posts. Rebounds, deflections, and balls off the post happen all the time. Stay with the play, and look to finish it off if the opportunity arises.

- If you're shooting, keep the ball down. Striking a shot that flies over the crossbar does absolutely nothing for your team. By keeping the shot low, several positive things can happen. The ball can go in the net, it can deflect off of a player, and it can rebound off the goalie or a post. You still have a chance to score in that situation. We scored a ton of goals off restarts at Carolina by keeping the shot low and framing the goal.

- If you have an indirect kick from twelve yards or closer, drill it on net around head-height. Most likely, it will deflect off of a player and go in the goal. The other option is to roll the ball to a teammate and have her fire a shot. I think your best bet is just to crank the ball at the wall. It's bound to hit something and go in the goal. If not, play the rebound. I like the idea of hitting it around head height because the defenders are all on the goal line, and it's frightening to try to save a shot from Shannon MacMillan from that close.

Long direct kicks. Fouls often occur thirty-five to forty yards away from the goal. Shooting the ball from this distance is not exactly a high-percentage shot. I'm sure it's been done successfully in the past, probably at lower levels, but more often than not it will be an easy save for the goalkeeper.

Have players make runs to cover all the significant areas in the box: the near post, far post, goalkeeper, six- and twelve-yard line. Runs should start before (not at) the defensive line so players can beat their opponent to the assigned spot. It's much harder to stay with a player who is running at you than if you both start from the same place.

As the player taking the free kick, drive the ball to an area away from the keeper's space. Because the ball is in front of the goalie, and

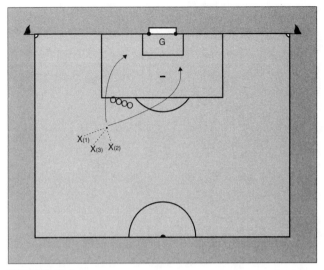

FIGURE 10.1
DIRECT KICK PLAY 1 (SHOT) – Players 1 and 2 run over the ball, and player 3 takes a shot. Players 1 and 2 continue their runs and frame the goal.

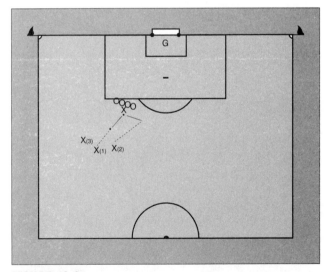

FIGURE 10.2
DIRECT KICK PLAY 2 (SHOT) – Player 1 sends a push pass to her teammate (X) positioned in the wall. Player 2 then breaks forward and to the right and receives a one-time pass from player X. Player 2 takes a shot. This play allows the shooter a clear shot at the goal.

Shooters have the option of chipping the ball over the wall, bending it around the wall, or blasting it at the wall.

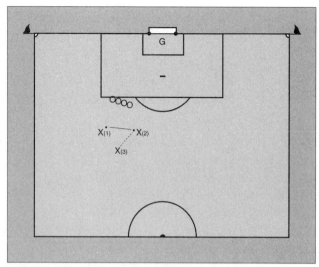

FIGURE 10.3
DIRECT KICK PLAY 3 (SHOT) – The ball starts with Player 1.
She sends a short ground pass to player 2. As the pass is played,
player 3 begins her approach to the ball. Player 2 receives the
pass, stops it for player 3 to come through and rip a shot. Again,
this play allows the shooter a clear shot at the goal.

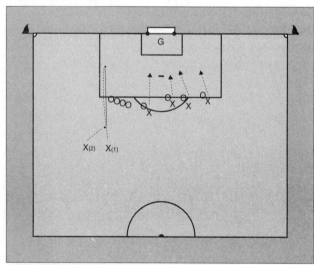

FIGURE 10.4
DIRECT KICK PLAY 4 (CROSS) – Player 1 runs over the ball and
continues her run off the left side of the wall. Player 2 bends a
pass to the left of player 1. Player 1 collects the ball on the run
and sends a cross to her teammates crashing the net.

not coming from her side (like a corner kick),
she's much more likely to come out and make a
play. Hit the ball away from her space and force
her to hold her line.

Penalty Kick

A penalty kick is awarded when a foul, which
ordinarily results in a direct free kick, occurs
within the offending team's penalty area. All
players except for the kicker and the opposing
goalkeeper must stand outside of the penalty
box and arc. The shooter places the ball on the
penalty mark, which is drawn twelve yards from
the center of the goal.

After a penalty kick is taken, any player
except the shooter can play the ball. The kicker
may not play the ball until it has been touched
or played by another player on either team.
That means if the ball hits off the post or crossbar, you can't follow your own shot. If the goalkeeper touches the ball, you can play the
rebound and shoot again. Remember my
penalty kick story!

A penalty kick provides a tremendous scoring opportunity. If you strike a good shot, the
goalkeeper doesn't have a chance. You hold the
advantage.

I've made a lot of penalty kicks in my day,
but I've also missed some. My best advice is to
know where you're going with your shot before
you walk up there to take the kick. Make the
decision in your mind, visualize the shot, and
simply execute. An indecisive approach or one
that lacks confidence will adversely affect your
shot. Overthinking in this situation can really
mess you up.

Decide which corner, how high, how hard,
what part of the foot, spin or no spin. You
might choose to push a shot to the right corner
with the inside of your foot or to drive a ball
with your instep to the left side. You have
to decide what shot feels most comfortable to
you. I can't tell you what that is. It's a matter of
personal preference. I either hit the ball with my

laces to the left or with the inside of my foot to the right. In case any girl reading this becomes a goalie in the WUSA, I'm not telling you which one. But I try to keep the ball low.

Goal Kicks

Just because you're in your defensive end, don't view goal kicks as a defensive play. It's your kick, so your team has possession of the ball. Your goal should be to get the ball out of the backfield while maintaining possession. Defenders will mark behind your players, so right there you already have an advantage to win the ball out of the air.

I consider a few things when taking a goal kick. If the opposing team has a player who is strong in the air, I keep it away from her. I try to hit the ball for distance, but at the same time, I drive the ball. My teammates will be trying to flick the ball, and it's easier to flick a ball that's driven.

Remember that you don't always have to kick your goal kicks as far as possible. You can pass the ball to a teammate right outside of the penalty box if she is open. This way, possession is guaranteed.

As Brandi sinks to her knees and raises her arms in victory, more than 90,000 spectators go berserk. The rest of us rush onto the field to celebrate winning the 1999 World Cup title.

The Shootout: World Cup 1999

Penalty kicks can be pretty tough to watch, but nothing compares with what it was like in the 1999 World Cup final. I was kneeling on the ground holding everyone else's hands on the sideline. I was just hoping we made all of ours. I didn't want any of our women to miss. And they didn't. They all nailed their shots.

When Brandi rifled that final shot, I just took off running. I can't tell you who I hugged or jumped on first. I just ran. The noise in that stadium was unbelievable. It was truly a moment I will never forget.

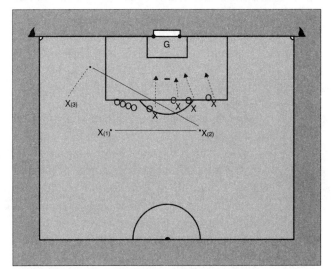

FIGURE 10.5
DIRECT KICK PLAY 5 (CROSS) – The ball starts with Player 1. Player 3 is positioned to the far left. Player 1 sends a ground pass to player 2. Player 2 sends a one-time pass to player 3 in the corner. Player 3 collects the ball and sends a cross to her teammates crashing the net. This play is designed so the defense shifts to the right on the initial pass, leaving open space for player 3 in the left corner.

Defensive Restarts

Playing defense on restarts isn't quite as exciting as offensive restarts, but it's equally important. Because the opponent now has a scoring opportunity, you've got to really concentrate on defending.

Corner Kicks

Here's your defensive approach on corner kicks. Cover all the danger areas, make sure everyone is marked up man-to-man, and get the ball out of there. Think of it this way. The offense has to win the ball and hit it on goal. The defense has to win the ball and hit it anywhere but the goal. Seems easier doesn't it?

Put one player on the inside of the near post and one on the inside of the far post. Have one player straddling the six-yard line and everyone else playing man to man, touching tightly, which means you're touching her wherever she goes. If she gets outside of your reach, she can accelerate. You need to be touch-tight to stay with her.

Stay goal side and ball side of your mark as she makes her run. When the ball is struck, maintain contact with your mark and find the ball. Get to the ball at its highest point and clear it to the side or upfield. Do not redirect the ball in toward the goal. Once the ball is cleared or under the goalkeeper's control, clear out of the box.

Anytime you hear the goalie call for the ball, get out. It's her ball. Don't continue to the ball because you may obstruct the goalkeeper from making the play. If she calls it, get out of her way. And be sure your mark doesn't hurt your goalkeeper.

Free Kicks

When a free kick is awarded and lies within scoring distance, immediately begin forming your wall. Players who stand in the wall should be chosen in practice. The game is not the time to deliberate. Rules state that the wall must be ten yards from the place of the kick, so line up about seven yards from the ball. Force the opponent to request ten yards from the referee. It buys time and allows your defense to get organized.

The distance from the goal and location of the ball dictates the number of players in your wall. If the origin of the foul is twenty-two yards out and in the center of the field, you'll probably have five players in your wall. If it's thirty-five yards out, you may only use three players. The goalkeeper usually makes the decision.

The wall. The object inside the wall is to stay connected. Don't move. Turning or ducking can cost your team a goal. If you saw Mia's goal off of a free kick for the Washington Freedom—the first goal an American woman scored in the WUSA—it was like the parting of the Red Sea. Mia hit the ball at the wall but the players in the wall turned and the keeper never had a chance. If they stayed connected, the shot would have been blocked.

Players in the middle of the wall often lock arms to eliminate any cracks in the wall. (Finally, a wall where I'm not in the line of fire.)

Listen to the goalkeeper when forming the wall. She will direct you to the right or to the left. She has the best view of the play and is counting on you to help her with her angle. Listen for her voice and do as she says.

As short as I am, I'm almost always in the wall. They either put me on the outside of the wall or have me rush the ball. That's called the kamikaze run and sets you up to take one in the face. Yeah, thanks for that job. I guess they figure I'm crazy enough for the job. I guess that's kind of a compliment.

All other defenders have to mark up tightly. Remember, deception is the key. They may fake a shot and push a pass to a player you may not expect to receive the ball. Play your mark touch-tight and don't get caught being a spectator.

A FAIR ASSESSMENT

Greg Fair
Brother

"One thing that I really like about Lorrie is what you see is what you get. And it's not just because she's my little sister. I think it's an admirable trait in the eyes of anyone who knows her. She doesn't put up any false fronts. She's unique as an athlete in that her personality on and off the field are pretty much the same. She's the type of person who always likes to have fun, she's very creative and very intense. Maybe there is a higher level of intensity on the field, but overall, her character traits off the field are consistent with the way she plays on the field."

"You're a much better soccer player when you're

in good shape, plain and simple."

Conditioning

Hey, at least I put this chapter toward the end of the book. I know a lot of you cringe when you hear conditioning, but if you keep an open mind and embrace it, you'll learn to enjoy it. It will transform from something you have to do to something you want to do. While conditioning is typically linked to physical health, it does wonders for your mental health as well.

Like it or not, conditioning is a major, major part of playing soccer. One thing I like about conditioning is it's something that is totally within your control. You can put forth the effort to get fit enough to play at your highest level, or you can avoid conditioning and allow it to hold you back. There are a number of variables in soccer that are out of your hands, but conditioning is completely up to you.

The Benefits of Fitness

Ideally, you want to be able to get yourself into condition so that you can sprint for ninety minutes. To do that, you have to build power and stamina. Soccer demands quickness and speed, but it also requires endurance. These skills are a product of your fast- and slow-twitch muscles. Fast-twitch muscles prompt players to quick explosive movements that are necessary to chase down a loose ball or make an overlapping run. In general, they are the muscle fibers that characterize sprint-type movements. Slow-twitch muscles allow for optimum performance in endurance-type activities. The ability to run throughout an entire game depends on slow-twitch muscles.

The capacity of your fast- and slow-twitch muscles is largely influenced by your genetic makeup. Some people are simply born to run faster or jump higher. However, your individual strengths (or weaknesses) can be improved through fitness training.

Being in shape greatly benefits your game. You can make runs all day, cover more ground, maintain fresh legs late in the game, and reduce your risk of injury. Your cuts will be sharper and more explosive, and you'll enhance your technical skill by avoiding fatigue.

Think about the advantage of being in better physical condition than your opponent. Late in

Anson Dorrance
UNC women's soccer head coach

"By the time she was a junior, Lorrie's fitness was extraordinary. She could paint the entire field during a game. She developed a great personal training program and had remarkable discipline in college. Lorrie never would fall victim to not working hard enough."

the game, she is worn out while you're firing on all engines. She'll have trouble keeping up with you, winning 50/50 balls, and will probably give you a bigger cushion to receive and handle the ball. Fitness can be the difference between winning and losing.

Being in great shape increases your value as an individual player, but when the entire team is in great shape it makes a significant difference. If I coached a team that was short on talent, I'd work hard to improve their skills, but I

Conditioning gives you the strength, quickness, and endurance to play hard for ninety minutes.

would also run them into the ground so we were the most fit team competing. We'd win games on fitness and mental toughness.

Failing to Condition

Playing in poor physical condition really hurts your game. Fatigue sets in, and your body begins to struggle to execute what your mind is telling it to do. Basic skills such as dribbling, receiving, passing, and shooting suffer as power, accuracy, and quickness are sacrificed. When fatigue sets in, the first thing I lose is my technique. What was once natural and effortless tends to break down because the muscles are too tired to work. Once this happens, I have to expend more energy to focus on the simple and basic skills, the ones that were once automatic.

Growing up, I played with a lot of girls who were exceptionally talented but didn't want to dedicate the time and energy to fitness. They were able to get away with it early on, but even then they weren't playing to their full potential for ninety minutes. Eventually, lack of conditioning caught up with them, and they became mediocre players. The good news is that it's easy to be a great player if fitness is all you're missing. You don't have to learn new skills, you just have to make the decision to get fit.

As you progress and reach higher levels of play, other girls will be just as talented. Perhaps the one thing that sets you apart is your fitness level. As we talked about in Chapter 1, soccer takes more than talent. It takes a willingness to commit and dedicate yourself both on and off the field. Like Anson used to tell us at Carolina, "It's what you do when no one's watching that makes you a champion."

So get yourself in shape to play soccer. You'll enhance your technical skill on the field, develop mental toughness, and feel great about yourself.

Total Fitness

Conditioning is not confined to running. To be the best soccer player you can be, you have to develop total fitness. Obviously, running is required, but there are a variety of other facets to conditioning. Balance, agility training, strength training, flexibility training, and nutrition are all integral to becoming a complete soccer player.

I know you may be hoping that I'll give you a personal-conditioning program to supplement your training. I'd love to devise a plan, but I can't possibly do that. Consider that each girl reading this book differs in age, height, weight, muscle development, body structure, ability, and purpose. It's simply not safe to devise a universal plan for everyone. To develop your own program, consult a certified trainer, a conditioning coach, or an accredited expert recommended by an experienced player.

I can explain why the different aspects of conditioning are important, how they're applied to soccer, and how to perform specific drills and exercises.

Balance

When you think about it, soccer is all about balance. Try dribbling, shooting, receiving, or passing off-balance. It's not going to happen, at least not effectively. Maintaining balance is dependent on traditional physical skills: flexibility, strength, and agility. Each is vital to keeping a sturdy foundation.

Core strength is important to developing balance. Core strength involves all the muscles around your center of gravity, the ones above your knees and below your chest. Your thighs, hip flexors, abductors, lower back muscles, abdominals, and glutes join together to give you core strength.

You can tell how much core strength a person has when you push her. People with a weak core are easily moved and can be pushed off the

Core strength is critical to basic soccer skills like shielding the ball from the defender.

ball. People who have strong cores will be tough to budge. When you're holding off a defender with the ball at your feet, it appears that you're using your arms, but you're actually using your core muscles to help protect the ball at your feet and keep your opponent at a distance.

Improving balance. Balance training is relatively new. It's difficult to fit into the practice schedule, so it's the type of training that you have to initiate on your own or with a friend. Soccer is a sport in which you develop balance just by playing; you are using your core and training those muscles with your movements on the field. But to really improve, you have to put in that extra time off the field.

The first step to improving balance is to increase your core strength. Strength exercises that isolate the core muscles build a solid foundation. These exercises are labeled later in this chapter. Use them to build and improve balance.

You can use several drills where both feet are on flat ground to get started. Squats, lunges, and diagonal lunges are simple exercises that develop balance. Put your weight on your heels and your feet flat. Focus on balance control as you squat down and push up, and as you lunge out with one leg and return to the starting position. Also, include quick feet drills with an emphasis on staying balanced. Stand on one side of a soccer ball, and step over to the other side. Continue doing step-overs, back and forth, as quickly as you can.

Next, try exercises that force you to balance on one leg. Stand on one leg and hold it for ten seconds. Hop up and switch to stand on the opposite leg. Pretend you're the Karate Kid.

Do single-leg squats and finish up by having a catch with a soccer ball, all the while standing on one leg. If you can toss and catch the ball on one leg, you have excellent balance.

When I want to increase the difficulty of these exercises, I use a half a cylinder made of foam and stand on top of the flat side. It's an unstable surface and makes it really tough to maintain balance. As you're doing it, you really feel all your core muscles working. I challenge you to find a more exhausting workout where you never move from one spot.

Performing exercises on an unstable surface is an advanced skill. Don't try it without approval and supervision. Participating in an exercise you're not ready for risks injury.

Agility

Soccer is a series of five-yard movements. You use bursts of speed and quick changes of direction to win balls and beat opponents. These types of movements require a combination of balance, quickness, explosive power, and agility. Agility is essential when you need to quickly steer your energy where you need it to go.

We had a track star play with us at Carolina. She could absolutely fly. We've got some fast girls on our team, but when we ran 120s (120-yard sprints), she came in first place pretty easily each time. Then, we put out cones for sprint drills that required change of direction. We ran a drill called a "jingle-jangle," in which you sprint ten times back and forth in a ten-yard area as fast as you can and try to record the fastest time. The track runner came in last place every time. She was like lightning running straight ahead, but she couldn't change direction.

The following are some simple drills to enhance your agility skills. It's important to perform them at maximum speed to elicit optimum production and results. Your body has to develop a sense of how to change direction and quickly accelerate while operating at game speed. Going through the motions accomplishes nothing.

Around the world. Many of you who've played basketball will recognize the name of this drill, but the soccer version entails a lot more running. It requires a goal, five cones, and a stopwatch. Cone 1 is placed on the middle of the goal line. Cone 2 is placed on the right corner of the six-yard line. Cone 3 is placed on the penalty kick line. Cone 4 is placed on the middle of the eighteen-yard line, and cone 5 is placed on the left corner of the six-yard line.

Starting from cone 1, the timer yells "go" and you take off. Touch the right goalpost and then return to touch cone 1. Run and touch cone 2 and return to touch cone 1. Turn and sprint to cone 3 on the penalty kick line and then return to touch cone 1. Continue the same process through cones 4 and 5 and finally the left goalpost. The clock stops when you touch cone 1 for the final time.

Keep track of your times, and strive to improve each session. To step things up a bit, go around the world and then return around the world in reverse order without stopping. Return by going to the left goalpost and then cones 5, 4, 3, 2, and finish with the right goalpost before touching cone 1. It's double the effort, but double the fun.

Four corners. Place four cones in a square that is twelve yards long by twelve yards wide. Start at the cone in the lower right-hand corner. Sprint forward to the cone in the upper right-hand corner. Carioca to the left across the top of the square. Your first step is a crossover step with your right foot over your left. Your left foot then slides behind your right foot. Your right foot then crosses behind your left foot and then your left foot swings in front of your right. So it's right foot crossover, left behind, right foot cross behind, left foot crossover. Keep your upper body facing forward and hold your arms out for balance. It may take a little while to establish a rhythm, but it's an excellent exercise for agility.

Then run backward down the left side of the square. Keep your eyes straight ahead and extend your legs back and outward as you run back. Your upper body remains erect—don't lean back—and be sure to pump your arms. Run straight back and . . . don't fall.

Finally, take shuffle steps across the bottom of the square. Spread your feet farther than shoulder-width apart, flex your knees, and bend at the waist. Shuffle to the right without crossing your feet. Don't stand up, stay low as you shuffle across.

Continue for four circuits around the square, rest for forty-five seconds, and repeat.

1. Sprint

2. Carioca (from right to left)

3. Run backward

4. Shuffle steps

Line jumps. Stand with two feet together and a chalk line on your right side. Jump over the line and land on the opposite side. Continue back and forth for thirty seconds keeping your feet together. Try to maximize your number of jumps in the allotted time.

To increase the difficulty of the drill, use a cone or soccer ball instead of a line. It forces you to jump higher.

A variation of this drill is to jump forward and backward. Start in back of the line and leap forward over it. Jump back and forth as many times as possible in thirty seconds. Use a cone or soccer ball to increase difficulty. When you really get good, try it on one leg.

Lateral jumps over the soccer ball improve leg strength, agility, and balance. A variation of lateral jumps is to jump forward and backward over the ball (right).

Dealing with a Serious Injury (Ronnie Fair)

"I suffered a terrible injury in March of my junior year in high school. I went up for a headball and landed sideways on my ankle. All I heard was this loud, crunching sound and I knew I had done some serious damage. I broke my leg, dislocated my ankle, and ended up having to get four screws and a pin put in my leg.

"I was afraid I'd never play again, that I would never bounce back. You never think something like that is going to happen to you, so you can't possibly be psychologically prepared when it does. The toughest thing was watching my friends and teammates playing. I felt abandoned. You quickly realize that the sport continues forward without you and it's a pretty harsh reality to absorb.

"Beside not being able to play, it was really tough because there was interest from several college coaches. Some were already recruiting me, and others were planning to see me play that summer. There was nothing worse than making that phone call and telling them what happened. As it turned out, all the coaches I spoke with were very supportive.

"When I began rehabilitating, I learned that your greatest asset is your attitude. If you stay positive and focus on simple goals, you'll recover faster. If you're pessimistic and focus on the frustration, your progress will suffer. Isolating yourself and wanting sympathy is not going to help. You have to set minigoals for yourself all the time and set your mind to achieving those goals. I can remember the first time I stretched with the Sunnyvale team at a tournament. I still couldn't play but I was totally psyched. It just felt so good to be out on the field with the girls.

"I played with a slight degree of uncertainty when I first came back. I was a little worried I'd reinjure my ankle if I played too aggressively. With time, I regained confidence in my leg. One positive I got out of it was that I learned to avoid senseless tackles.

"Overall, the injury helped me to grow as a person. Before the injury, I was a soccer player. That was my identity. Once that was taken away for a period of time, it gave me greater perspective. I was able to enjoy other things outside of sports. My college experience couldn't have worked out better. I went to Stanford University, played for four years, and loved every minute of it. I'm still a soccer player today with the New York Power, but I know there are so many other things out there whenever I decide to hang up my cleats."

Ball touches. Stand directly in front of a soccer ball and rest the ball of your right foot on top of the ball. This is the starting position. At the sound of a whistle or coach's call, interchange your feet as quickly as possible. Repeatedly exchange your feet, touching the top of the ball with the balls of your feet—left, right, left, right, left, right, and so forth. Continue exchanging feet for thirty seconds, accumulating as many touches as possible. Keep track of your total number and attempt to beat that number each time out. This exercise works on improving foot speed while maintaining balance.

Flexibility Training

Stretching is definitely an area that I have to improve. I need to stretch more. Sometimes I think I'm still under the impression that I'm eight years old and can hop out of the car and start running top speed. That used to be the

Exchange feet touching the top of the soccer ball to enhance your foot speed and agility.

case, but now, I'd hear a bunch of cracks and pops before my first foot hit the pavement.

First and foremost, stretching reduces the risk of injury. Don't be the victim of a foolish injury because you didn't spend enough time stretching. Take it from me, being injured and unable to play is no fun. I had problems with my hamstring during my first year with the Philadelphia Charge and even had to miss some games. I have to constantly be attentive to my hamstrings and make sure they're loose. If I don't, they'll tighten up and I'll strain or, even worse, pull one. I stretch before and after workouts, and you should do the same. After each initial stretch, relax and then stretch the same muscle again. You will find that you can stretch a little farther the second time through.

Flexibility also helps your game. If you can reach that extra inch to win the ball or put your body in a strange, but still powerful position to make a play, you're more productive. Being flexible is a quiet commodity that can pay big dividends.

These stretching exercises start from the ankles and move upward. Refer to this routine before workouts, practices, and games.

Ankle stretch. Lift your foot off the ground and balance on one leg. Point your toe toward the ground and make circles with your foot to loosen the ankle joint. Make ten circles and

Stretching before the game is essential, but it's also a great time to loosen up mentally by joking with your teammates.

The calf and Achilles tendon stretch

then switch feet. After completing two sets of ten, make counterclockwise circles with your feet ten times.

Calf and Achilles tendon stretch. Squat, lean forward, and place your hands flat on the ground in front of you. Extend your right leg back and put the ball of your right foot on the ground. Lift your left foot and rest it on the heel of your right foot. As you attempt to lower your right heel to the ground, you'll feel your calf muscle stretch. Hold the stretch for ten seconds and then switch legs. Continue until you stretch each leg three times (three sets).

Upper hamstring stretch. Lay flat on your back. Bend your left leg at the knee and raise it toward your midsection. Grab the shin of your left leg with both hands and pull into your midsection. Pull your knee toward your chin as far as possible. Your right leg and back should remain flat on the ground. Hold the stretch for ten seconds and then switch legs. Complete three sets for each leg. After completing the first stage of this stretch, take it one step further and extend your leg upward so the sole of your foot faces the sky. Grab your calf with both hands and pull your leg in toward your chest. Try to keep your opposite leg flat on the ground.

I've had problems in the past with my hamstrings, so I make sure I spend ample time getting them loose and limber before competing.

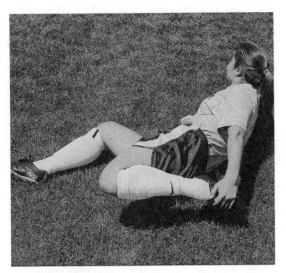

The quadriceps stretch

The groin stretch

Lower hamstring stretch. Spread your feet out wide in the standing position. Bend at your waist to the right and grab your ankle with both hands. (If you're flexible enough to grab your foot, that's even better!) Hold the stretch for ten seconds and then switch over to your left leg. Continue until you stretch each leg three times (three sets).

Quadricep stretch. Lie on the ground and rest on your right side. Bend your left knee back and grab your ankle with your left hand. Pull your left leg behind you so the heel of your left foot touches your rear end. Hold the stretch for ten seconds; then lie on your left side and stretch your right leg. Stretch each quadriceps three times.

Groin stretch. Squat in a baseball catcher's position and place your palms on the ground in front of you. Press your elbows inside your knees and lean forward. Use your hands to maintain your balance and hold the stretch for ten seconds. Relax and then repeat three times.

Torso stretch. Sit on the ground with your legs stretched outward in front of you. Bend your

The torso stretch

right leg at the knee, slide your right foot inward toward your buttocks, and grab your right knee with both hands. Next, lift your right foot over your left leg and place it on the outside of your left knee. Put your right hand on the ground by your right side (for balance) and place your left hand on the outside of your right knee. Pull the knee to the left to feel a stretch in the right portion of your torso. Hold for ten seconds and switch.

Stretching out the abdominal muscles

Lower back stretch. Lie flat on your stomach on the ground. Use both hands to push your upper body up off the ground, but keep your entire lower body (from the waist down) pressed against the ground. Hold this position for ten seconds and then rest. Repeat this four or five times to stretch the lower back.

Weight Training

Long gone are the days when girls wouldn't enter the weight room. I think Brandi showed us all in quite convincing fashion. We consider ourselves athletes and the bottom line is a stronger athlete can be a better athlete.

I'm not saying to go to the gym seven days a week and become a muscle head. You can't just lift weights and expect to get better on the soccer field. Combine it with agility drills, flexibility training, and improving your soccer skills. As you strengthen your muscles, train them for specific reasons. Teach your muscles the movements that you'll need on the field. Do squat exercises so you can jump higher for headballs, lunges so you're able to explode to the ball faster, side raises so you can better hold off defenders. Strength training is only beneficial on the soccer field if it's performed with a purpose.

Strength Exercises

There are many types of strengthening exercises, far too many to explore in this book. If you discover a program that includes exercises you don't recognize (or that are not described here), speak with a certified trainer and request that they show you the proper technique. To stress my point that your core muscles are extremely important when strengthening your body for competitive soccer, I've included the word "core" after the names of the exercises that contribute to the development of those muscles.

Leg extensions: quadricep muscles (core). Seated on a leg-extension machine, hook the tops of your feet under the pads. Lock your ankles, but don't point your toes. Extend your legs up so your thighs are flexed and your toes point to the ceiling. Slowly lower the weight back down until it's just short of the starting position. This keeps pressure on your legs throughout the exercise. Continue for ten to fifteen repetitions.

Leg curls: hamstring muscles (core). Lying face down on your stomach, lock your heels under the pads of the machine. Point your toes to the ground. Contract your glutes and curl your legs up as far as you can. Isolate the hamstrings by keeping your hips and chest down on the bench. Lower the weight slowly just short of the starting position. Continue for ten to fifteen repetitions.

Lunges: gluteus maximus muscles (core). With your arms down by your side, stand erect with your feet shoulder-width apart. Take a forward stride approximately three feet in distance. As your stride lands, bend your knee and lower your rear knee almost to the floor. Be careful not to let your knee extend farther than your toes. Push yourself back up to the starting position and repeat with the right leg. Continue for eight to ten repetitions.

To increase the difficulty of this exercise, hold dumbbells in each hand. Start off using dumbbells that are approximately five to ten pounds in weight.

Squat: lower back, quadriceps, and hamstring muscles (core). Holding either dumbbells or a straight bar on your shoulders, spread your feet slightly farther than shoulder-width apart. Stand with your weight on your heels, feet flat on the ground, and your head up. Keeping your upper body erect, slowly squat straight down until your rear end is at an equal level with your knees. Stop and push straight upward, keeping your upper body erect, eyes and chest facing forward. Continue for ten repetitions at a slow pace.

Bent-leg sit-ups: abdominal muscle (core). Lying on your back, bend your knees in and place the soles of your feet on the ground. Place your hands behind your head and curl up bringing your chest up to your knees. Continue for twenty to twenty-five repetitions.

A FAIR ASSESSMENT

Julie Foudy

U.S. women's soccer team captain

"Lorrie will eat anything. Do you remember that Life cereal commercial? 'Give it to Mikey. He'll eat anything.' Well, that's Lorrie for us on the national team. When we travel to different countries and there's some strange food on the table, we just yell out, 'Fair, try it.' The only problem is, she's not a real good gauge because she likes everything. The last time we were in China, she ate chicken feet. She's like, 'It's good!'

"I think we need to find another taste tester."

Bent-leg sit-up twists: abdominal muscles (core). Lie flat in the bent-leg sit-up position. As you curl up, twist so your left elbow touches your right knee. Lower yourself back down and alternate by touching your right elbow to your left knee. Continue for fifteen to twenty repetitions.

Medicine ball hand-offs: torso and abdominal muscles (core). You'll need a partner for this exercise. Holding a medicine ball, stand back to back with your partner. Twist to the right as your partner twists to her left and hand her the ball. Immediately twist to the left and receive a pass back from your partner. After approximately fifteen exchanges, switch directions and pass the ball off to your left.

V-seat pull-ins: lower back muscles (core). Sitting on a universal weight machine, extend your legs out in front of you and place the soles of your feet up against the footplates. Lean forward with your upper body to grab the handle grips with both hands. Return to the seated position and allow your knees to flex slightly. Pull the grips into your midsection and stick your chest out as your arms touch your midsection. Slowly allow the weight to return to the starting position.

Pull-downs: upper back muscles. Seated on the pull-down machine, grab the ends of the bar with both hands, palms facing forward. Tilt your head slightly forward and pull the bar down behind your head until it touches your neck. Let the bar slowly rise back up and then pull back down. Continue for ten to fifteen repetitions. To alter the exercise and isolate upper back muscle region, flip your hands so that your palms face you. Pull the bar down in to the top of your chest and slowly return it to the starting position. Continue for ten to fifteen repetitions.

Bench press: pectoral muscles. Lie flat on a weight bench with your feet flat on the ground. Grip the bar so your middle knuckles are pointed up to the ceiling. Each hand should be approximately three to four inches outside your shoulder. Lift the bar off of the rack and hold it over your chest. Slowly lower the bar until it touches the upper region of your chest. Keep your elbows under the bar. Push the bar back up until near extension. Continue for ten to fifteen repetitions.

Bicep curls: bicep muscles. Seated on the edge of a bench, hold a dumbbell in each hand. Rotate your wrists outward so your palms face forward. While maintaining an erect posture, slowly curl the dumbbell up near your collarbone. Lower the dumbbell back down and repeat the movement with your opposite arm. Repeat this ten to fifteen times with each arm.

Tricep pull-downs: tricep muscles. Standing at a pull-down machine, grasp the bar with both hands spread slightly narrower than shoulder-width apart. Use a forward grip so your palms face the floor. Push straight down on the bar until your arms nearly lock. Slowly let the bar return to the starting position. Continue for ten to fifteen repetitions.

Side shoulder raise: shoulder muscles. Stand straight up with your arms hanging down by your sides. Holding a light dumbbell in each hand, raise your arm out and up until it's parallel with the ground. When the dumbbell is at shoulder height, your palms should face the ground. Allow the dumbbell to slowly return to the starting position and raise the opposite arm. Continue each arm for ten to fifteen repetitions.

Nutrition

The first thing I would say about nutrition is to drink a lot of water. Drink more than you would think, especially if you sweat a lot. The last thing you want is to become dehydrated. Fluids act as your body's cooling system, and you need to replenish fluids as you exercise and

Make sure you drink plenty of water before, during, and after practice and games.

FOOD GROUP	MAJOR NUTRIENTS	DAILY SERVINGS
Dairy	Calcium, protein, vitamin A, riboflavin	3 servings
One serving is 8 ounces of milk, 8 ounces of yogurt, 1 ½ ounces of cheese		
Meat/Poultry	Protein, thiamin, riboflavin, iron, niacin, zinc	2–3 servings
One serving is 3 ounces of lean meat (poultry, pork, fish, beef), 2 eggs, 1 cup of cooked beans or peas, 4 tablespoons of peanut butter		
Fruit and Vegetable	Vitamins A and C and many other vitamins and minerals	5–7 servings
One serving is ½ cup of cooked vegetables, ½ cup of chopped vegetables, 1 whole fruit (apple, orange, banana), ½ grapefruit, 6 ounces of juice, ½ cup of berries		
Bread and Pasta	Complex carbohydrates, protein, B vitamins, iron	6–11 servings
One serving is 1 slice of bread, ½ English muffin, 1 small roll or biscuit, ½ cup of cooked rice or pasta, 1 ounce of breakfast cereal.		

compete. Drink plenty of water or sports drinks before, during, and after workouts and competition. If you see me at halftime, my jersey is usually soaked through. I try to change into a new jersey, but when I can't I am a dripping mess by the end of the match. I had people ask me why my jersey was a different color than everyone else's at Carolina.

I kind of equate diet to stretching. When you're younger, you don't worry about either, but as you get older, they become important. I'm a proponent of getting the right foods in you, but I don't think you have to completely cut out all fast foods or sweets. I still eat cheeseburgers and pizza, and I love ice cream. I just don't eat any of these foods in excess or before competition. If you eat the right things and get the nutrients your body needs, there's nothing wrong with indulging a little and treating yourself. Just make sure you save a little for me.

Eating Before Games

I think about what I eat the night before a game. I consume meals that will generate energy for the next day, food that has a lot of protein, carbohydrates, and minerals. I'll have a solid meal and maybe snack on something later at night.

A critical point to keep in mind the day of a game is to eat foods that are easily digestible. Don't eat a big steak at one o'clock when you have a game at five. It takes too long to break down the steak and your body will expend energy digesting instead of being primed for competition. Complex carbohydrates such as pasta, baked potatoes, toast, and cereals work well. Keep the portions small so that your meal is easily digested.

Do not eat foods that contain a lot of fat and avoid sugary foods as well. Fats are digested at

Tiff Milbrett might be fast on the field, but no one is as quick as I am with a fork and a knife.

a much slower rate and can make you feel sluggish. (A little bit of fat is good because in a ninety-minute game, fat is needed for stamina.)

Sweets such as candy bars, soda, or honey may raise your blood-sugar level and reduce your energy level.

For the most part, learn what your body responds positively to. Your body is unique, so you have to find a formula that works for you. Some people can eat two hours before the game, while others need four hours. Some girls like a granola bar and others eat a hoagie. Experiment until you find what you're comfortable eating, and when you do, just make sure you get enough nutrients and plenty of fluids.

To maintain a balanced diet, use the four basic food groups as your guideline. A combination of foods from the dairy group, meat and poultry group, fruit and vegetable group, and bread and pasta group provides a basic structure from which to devise your dietary plan. The table on page 161 lists the food group, the major nutrients each supplies, and the recommended amount for teenage athletes.

"It Ain't Easy Being Cheezy"

When I trained with the national team during my senior year of high school, we trained in Orlando, Florida. It was my first extended time away from home and my eating habits were a little on the undisciplined side.

In my own defense, I grew up eating everything in sight as fast as I could. If you didn't keep up, the food would be all gone. But it was all nutritious food. My parents didn't keep any junk food in the house. Like Pooh said, Friday night was pizza night and that was a huge deal in my family.

It was considered junk food night.

When I went away, I was introduced to a whole new world of junk food. I went from Cheerios in the morning to Fruit Loops and Cap'n Crunch. I lived on grilled cheese sandwiches at night, and I think I was eating Cheetos every free moment I had. I ate more Cheetos during those six months than most people eat in a lifetime. No one ever told me you didn't have to finish the bag. In my house, you finished what you started—house rule.

Empty-plate syndrome is what I called it.

I learned quickly that if you eat the wrong foods in large quantities, you're not going to be fit no matter how hard you train. I eat a lot smarter now. I make sure I get the proteins, carbohydrates, vitamins, and minerals that my body needs to perform. I still enjoy the things we all crave, though. Life is too short not to enjoy the finer things. I still eat Cheetos. It's just that when I open a bag, it has greater life expectancy than it used to.

"I can't imagine doing anything else
that I would enjoy more than being
a professional soccer player."

The Life

Congratulations! You made it! No more talking about push passes, thigh traps, or game strategy. As important as that information is, you deserve to kick back and read a little inside scoop on what it's like to play professional soccer. It still sounds strange to even say that, but believe it or not, I'm earning my living playing soccer! You've put your time in reading useful tips and advice on how to play the game, now it's time for you to enjoy reading about the life of a professional soccer player.

Despite much of the public's perception, being a professional athlete entails a lot more than playing in front of crowds and endorsement deals. A lot of responsibilities come with it. But I'll tell you what, there is nothing better. I get to be outside all the time, and I'm doing what I love most. I've traveled all over the world, been on the "Late Show with David Letterman," gone to Super Bowls thanks to Gatorade, received Nike apparel through my endorsement contract, and even appeared on MTV's "Road Rules." Yes, there are some time-consuming demands that come with the territory, but the bottom line is that there's nothing I'd rather be doing.

T.C.B.: Taking Care of Business

While there are a lot of exciting things that come with being a pro athlete, you have to make sure that your primary focus remains on being an athlete. You can't rely on what got you where you are, you've got to continue to push yourself to go further. That means taking care of yourself, maintaining fitness, striving to improve, and preparing for competition. Simply stated, you have to take care of business.

I know you've probably heard the word *responsibility* a thousand times from your parents, but you really have to take responsibility for yourself when playing pro sports. You have a responsibility to yourself, your teammates, and the organization. When it's thirty degrees outside and you have to run your fitness, it's you who has to go outside and do the work. No one else is there to enforce discipline. Players in the WUSA are not professionals because we're given great talent. It's what we do with that talent.

A day at the office

I constantly make sure I'm drinking enough water, eating the right foods for competition, taking care of my body, and getting enough rest. When making decisions, I consider what will help my performance on the field and what may adversely affect my game. It's pretty simple to see right from wrong when making those choices. I just make sure I'm conscious of my career at all times.

Injuries

The level of play in the WUSA is obviously a step up from college, but one of the biggest differences between being a pro soccer player and a collegiate athlete is dealing with injuries. In college, coaches preach that you're responsible for your injuries, but it really doesn't cost you when you're sidelined. Sure, you go nuts when you're unable to play, but you're still able to go to class. The main reason I went to college at Carolina was to get my degree. Injuries never stopped me from attending class.

Today, soccer is my livelihood. If I'm hurt, I can't play and can't excel on the field to help the team. I'm in risk of losing my job. It's pretty cutthroat in professional sports. No one cares about what you've done in the past. What are the lyrics to that Janet Jackson song? "What have you done for me lately?" A player who is constantly injured is in danger of losing her roster spot.

I've also become more attentive to what my body is telling me when confronted by nagging injuries. I'll give you an example. At the first day of 2002 camp with the Philadelphia Charge, we had testing. Coaches evaluate each player for speed, agility, leaping ability, and strength. Basically, they're interested in who came to camp in shape and who slacked during the off-season. I had a slight groin pull but told myself the night before that there was no way I was going to miss the first day of camp.

When I got out on the field, I knew my body didn't feel right. My instinct was to grit my teeth and tough it out. But I listened to my head instead of my heart. If I pushed my body during testing (which would have been inevitable), I may have pulled my groin. If that had happened, I would have been out four to six weeks and I'd be no good to anyone. So I spoke with the coaches and we decided it was best that I shut things down for the day.

I hated not being able to test with the team. I was in such good shape. I have a lot of personal pride that I'm the type of player who will play through an injury. But with it being preseason, the wise decision was to give myself a little more time to heal before going full throttle. Sometimes you have to think long term and do what is best for you and the team.

The WUSA Allocation and Draft

The evolution of the Women's United Soccer Association was a dream come true for so many people. I am extraordinarily grateful to all the women (and men) who laid the groundwork for the league to become a reality. In a perfect world, every woman who gave her heart and soul to the game of soccer would be granted some time on the field during a WUSA game. They deserve to run out on the field and hear the crowd.

The twenty roster players from the 1999 World Cup team are the founding members of the WUSA. The WUSA executive committee decided to allocate the twenty players around the league. That means that instead of being drafted, we were equally dispersed among the eight WUSA organizations. With Michelle Akers being injured, the number of players to be allocated was nineteen, so the league decided to add five more big-name players and distribute twenty-four players to eight teams (three per team).

Michelle ended up retiring and never played in the WUSA. She was truly the total package: smart, tenacious, skilled, and possessed a thunderous shot that will be talked about in the women's game for a long, long time. Her talents were extraordinary alone, but the fact that she performed them with Epstein-Barr syndrome and after countless surgeries is truly miraculous. She finally retired from the national team after shoulder surgery in 2001.

For all that Michelle sacrificed on the field, my biggest wish is that she could play in the WUSA. She is a symbol of U.S. women's soccer and is one of the greatest ambassadors of the sport. Michelle was an inspiration to me and a lot of the national team players, and the opportunity to play with her was an absolute blessing.

The league requested that the founding members list their top three choices as to where we'd like to play. They were hoping to satisfy the players, especially those who had families like Joy Fawcett (husband and three children in San Diego) and Carla Overbeck (husband and child in North Carolina). I had Philadelphia on my list, and received word that I was heading to the City of Brotherly Love. I've really enjoyed living and playing in Philadelphia. The cold winters I could do without, but the fans and the city have been great. The first time my brother, Greg, visited he came with some friends and we all ran up the steps to the Art Museum vintage Rocky Balboa.

After the twenty-four players were allocated, each team drafted a pair of foreign players. Organizations then contacted other foreign players to sign them individually, but a maximum of four foreign players is allowed on each team. Once the foreign players were placed on teams, the draft went to the players from around the country that were invited to a combine (a workout camp), where their skills were tested. They were selected in a regular draft format (first round, second round, and so forth). Each organization had preseason tryouts and camps to finalize their rosters. And on April 14, 2001, the Washington Freedom hosted the Atlanta Beat in the inaugural WUSA contest. Washington came out on top 1–0 and did so in storybook style. The lone goal was scored by Mia Hamm.

The WUSA is truly a dream come true for a pair of twin sisters from Los Altos, California.

Image

I'm conscious of the image I portray in public to an extent, but not for business reasons. I want to make sure I set a good example for young girls. I know when I was younger I was impressionable and tried to emulate people I looked up to. When I was a kid, there weren't many female athletes to idolize, so I idolized my dad. I used to do whatever he did.

I love interacting with kids because they're so wide open to new ideas. They're so attentive and absorb even the littlest thing like sponges.

Me, Brandi Chastain, Tisha Venturini, and Tiffany Roberts. As Brandi shows, it's always good to have a pen in hand.

What you illustrate to them can influence who they are, how they act, or what they aspire to be.

At times, I have had to remind myself to be careful of what I blurt out on the field. I think you know what I mean. I get caught up in the heat of battle and some words or terms may leave my tongue before being filtered through the brain. (Don't tell my mom.) If kids hear something that they shouldn't from a pro player, they're going to think that it's acceptable language, and that's not the message we want to convey. I'm not saying we're a bunch of truck drivers out there, but occasionally things can slip out in competition.

Having a Bad Day

When I'm not playing soccer, I'm just like any other twenty-four-year-old woman. I have bad days just like anyone else. Some days I'm tired, I don't feel well, I have a friendly disagreement over the phone, and I have to do an appearance. I have trouble hiding my emotions in my personal life, but feel I have a responsibility to be in good spirits if I'm meeting with children and fans.

A good asset to have is the ability to compartmentalize. That means that I take "bad-mood Lorrie" and place her in the closet for the afternoon. I take "pleasant, upbeat Lorrie" off the hanger and bring her to the function. While I am guilty of harboring human emotions, there are kids expecting me to be as happy to see them as they are to see me. So I leave my bad mood behind and focus on the kids.

Our national team sports psychologist, Colleen Hacker, taught us the trick "fake it till you make it." If you're having a horrible day, force yourself to walk around with a smile. Inevitably, people will start smiling back at you or make comments and it becomes kind of funny. Before long, you're laughing at yourself, and your day is turned around.

All That Comes with the Territory

While I've already said that your primary focus as a pro athlete is to prepare and play your sport to the best of your ability, a number of peripheral elements are part of the package. Most of them are very enticing, which is why I keep stressing that you remind yourself of your objectives at all times. If you get caught up in the lifestyle, your game—that is, what got you there—will begin to slip.

Travel

There is no question that travel has been a major bonus to my soccer career. With the WUSA, I obviously travel to New York, Washington, Boston, North Carolina, Atlanta, San Diego, and San Francisco. Those are all cool places to visit, and I've got friends in every town. But with the national team, the sites on the schedule are a bit more exotic.

During my tenure with the U.S. national and Olympic teams, I've played in China, Brazil, Norway, Mexico, Canada, Portugal, Australia, France, Germany, Sweden, the Netherlands, Denmark, and Japan. Most of our time is spent in the hotel or on the soccer field. The coaches do a pretty good job of allowing us a day or two to sightsee, but the number-one priority is winning, and that has to be our main focus.

When I do retire, I'm going everywhere I possibly can go. My friends and family can come with me. Traveling with soccer has shown me that there is so much out there, and I'd really like to experience different cultures and environments as a regular traveler and not just a visiting athlete.

Fair is Fair

I was training one time with one of my best friends who played on the men's U-17 national team, Alberto Montoya. He was absolutely drilling me into the ground. I was getting so upset because he was just kicking my tail in one on one. Finally I stopped and yelled, "This isn't fair! I'm having the most horrible day, and you're making it worse by beating me every, single time. You're not even giving me a chance!"

Do you know what his reply was? He said, "Lorrie, I don't care how your day has been up until now. Make it a good day!"

I'll always remember that. It was a great lesson to learn. No one really cares how your day has been, especially your opponents. So if it's 11 a.m. and your day has been terrible, what are you going to do the rest of the day? Mope? You have thirteen more hours to do with as you please.

Get on with your life. There's no point in dwelling on how miserable your day has been. I'd rather be happy.

And by the way, if you are having a bad day, stay away from Alberto.

A group of American athletes before the opening ceremonies at the 2000 Olympics in Sydney, Australia. We're looking pretty slick, wouldn't you say?

Some Fair Questions to Ask

Q: What keeps you motivated during hard times on the field?

LF: *Love for the game, ambition, and determination to reach my goals*

Q: What's the best piece of advice you would give younger girls who aspire to become professional athletes?

LF: *Let your passion for the game be your motivation and always play with heart.*

Q: If you could change one thing about yourself, what would it be?

LF: *My height, but only to add two or three inches*

Q: What do you do before a game to get psyched?

LF: *I listen to relaxing R&B music to get my mind to relax and I have a routine to putting on my gear.*

Q: What's your favorite flavor of ice cream?

LF: *Jamoca or coffee and cookies and cream*

Q: What do you look for most in an ideal mate?

LF: *Loyalty, honesty, sense of humor, outgoing*

Q: Do you plan on getting married and having a family?

LF: *I'd like to get married and have four children, but not right now.*

Q: Who was your inspiration while you were growing up?

LF: *My father*

Q: What do you do to get away from all the stresses of everyday life?

LF: *Go out to dinner, see a movie, go out dancing, sit and people-watch, do crosswords.*

All right, I'll admit it. We get to have some fun when we travel. I got to showcase my fishing skills in Tromso, Norway, and was all smiles after catching this fish.

Flying

And right after I tell you I love traveling, this will sound like it makes no sense at all; I don't like flying. It's not so much a fear of flying, but rather my body doesn't respond well to air travel. My ankles swell from sitting for long periods of time and flying at high altitudes. Luckily, I'm pretty "compact" so I can elevate my feet and hopefully fall asleep.

It's impossible to sleep for the entire flight on some of our national team flights. It takes fourteen hours to fly to China and twelve hours to fly back. Usually I'll bring a book to read or do any crossword puzzle I can get my hands on. My favorite book is *The Power of One* by Bryce Courtenay. I also bring music and recently bought a portable DVD player, which is awesome. I can watch my own movies on the flight.

Signing Autographs

I love signing autographs. I think it has some intrinsic value. I know if there were women's professional soccer players when I was a kid, I would have been so excited to get an autograph. The ultimate autograph I could have received as

Caught red-handed doing a crossword puzzle in the morning

A FAIR ASSESSMENT

David Bober
Lorrie's agent

"Lorrie is a special athlete and a special person. She has accomplished so much on and off the field. There are no limitations to what she can do when she puts her mind to it. As a player, Lorrie is very determined and is the quintessential team player. As a person, she's everything you'd ever want in a daughter. I feel very fortunate to have her as a client and to call her my friend."

a kid would have been one from Joe Montana. (If you're reading this, Joe, it's not too late.)

All of us on the Charge stay after games to sign autographs for kids in the stands. It feels so good to see a kid's face light up just by signing your name. You can really make an impact and that's a special feeling. And it's not just that we're doing something for the fans. It's a way for us to thank them for supporting our team and women's soccer. I'll sign anything a person gives me, within reason of course.

Hiring an Agent

After we won the World Cup in 1999, things were really hectic. The agents were going crazy sorting through endorsement offers and appearances for our national team players. I went back to UNC, so I avoided most of the chaos. I still had a year of collegiate eligibility, and if I accepted money that was affiliated with soccer, I would have lost my final year of eligibility. But I knew I was going to get an agent once my collegiate career was over.

I met a lot of agents through people on the national team and decided to hire David Bober of Bober Associates, Incorporated (BAI). He's

my agent, but he's also my friend and I love him to death. He really looks out for me and my best interests.

Dave is also the bad guy for me. He goes to battle for me when it comes time to negotiate contracts. He fields all offers for endorsement deals and appearances and sort of acts as a career advisor.

Dave also markets me as an individual. If there is something I want to pursue, whether it be career-oriented or doing work for a charity, he initiates contact and makes things happen. Marla Mullen and Dan Levy are two of Dave's associates, and they are great as well. It's great being a client at BAI because we have an excellent working relationship, but we also have a friendship. It's important that you trust the people you work with.

Many people wonder why athletes need agents, however, I think they're very helpful. If I spent my spare time fielding calls and working out contracts, it would take my focus away from my profession—training for and playing soccer. I wouldn't say they're an absolute necessity, but Dave and the gang have made my life a little easier.

Endorsements

Endorsement contracts allow athletes to earn money outside of their playing contract. You may wear specific apparel or speak on behalf of a company to promote their products.

My biggest endorsement contract is with Nike. I signed with them after I graduated from North Carolina and later restructured my deal with them after the 2000 Olympics in Sydney.

Basically, anytime I appear somewhere in public, I have to wear Nike apparel. I'm a representative of Nike, and they want me outfitted in their products. And they send me everything. I have Nike shirts, shorts, socks, footwear, towels, sweats, jackets, and even a set of Nike golf clubs. You name it and they've got it.

Things can get a little confusing when your team is sponsored by a company. The U.S. women's national team is sponsored by Nike, so it works out well for me. But there are other girls on the team who are endorsed by companies like Adidas or Fila. The rule is that when they're playing for the national team, they have to wear Nike products from the socks up. They can wear shoes of the company that personally endorses them.

The U.S. national team is endorsed by Nike.

The Philadelphia Charge is sponsored by Diadora (in 2002). So I wear Diadora apparel from the socks up, but my shoes are Nike. It works the same if I'm doing an appearance. If it's a function for the Charge, I wear Diadora with Nike shoes, but anything outside the WUSA I wear Nike from head to toe.

Wow, I'm tired out from just explaining that.

My Nike contract states that they can call me up to ten times per year to do appearances. Most of my appearances consist of fun activities. We sometimes speak at clinics or sign autographs at the mall. Could you imagine being paid to go to the mall? Talk about a dream coming true!

One of my appearances for Nike was to be on MTV's "Real World/Road Rules Challenge" with Sarah Whalen. Their challenge was to play human foosball. We trained the cast members for a soccer game. It was a lot of fun. There was some sort of romance drama going on between a member from the "Real World" team and one from "Road Rules." It was pretty funny.

Some other companies I've had endorsement deals with are Hershey, Welch's, and Nair to name a few. The Nair promotion was a contest where the winner was flown to Texas for a soccer clinic. So when the winner was announced and the date was set, I flew to Texas to participate in the clinic.

Photo Shoots

I think I'd rather run fitness than become a Hollywood entertainer. Photo and commercial shoots are a true test of patience. I'm a very active person, so maybe I'm not the best measure, but the amount of standing around you do in shoots takes more time and energy than running up and down a soccer field.

I'll do most magazine or commercial shoots because it helps promote the game. It also allows people to see you as a person and not just "that girl who tackles hard." It's another way to get in touch with the public. It's always fun to get photographed, but the amount of time it takes to get the shot just right can be lengthy.

The High Life

I love playing soccer and there are things outside of soccer that I enjoy doing to promote the sport. But there are some functions and events that I've been to or participated in that have been just plain awesome.

If winning the World Cup in 1999 didn't hit us down on the field that day, it certainly did in the days and weeks after. The events and appearances were nonstop. We went on every morning show like "Today" and "Good Morning America." Of course, we went on the "Late Show with David Letterman." Letterman kind of adopted us throughout our World Cup run and had us on as guests after winning.

We pulled up in a bus at a Bruce Springsteen concert in New Jersey a couple days after the final. The crowd started cheering because they thought it was Bruce and his band. We all started getting off and the crowd kind of got quiet because they saw a bunch of women filing out. Then they realized it was the U.S. women's national team and erupted. It was really funny. Springsteen made an announcement to the crowd that we were there and congratulated us. I'll never forget that night.

Of all the events and appearances I've attended, the one that takes the cake was my trip to Super Bowl XXXVI with Gatorade. Growing up with yard lines painted on my street, I have always been a huge football fan. Gatorade has invited me to attend their functions and the game as one of their representatives since Super Bowl XXXV.

Anyone would enjoy the trip and all the events that it includes. But because I'm a football fanatic and

Fair is Fair

I love being a representative of Nike. They're a great company. They were going to send me to Indonesia, Vietnam, and India to check out the Nike factories, but the trip was cancelled because of the September 11th attacks. I have visited two Nike factories in China. My biggest impression of the workplace was how spotless it was. The factories were extremely clean. I thought the working conditions were extremely good.

Watching them make shoes was an absolutely amazing experience. If you saw it, it would blow you away. Every time I see a Nike shoe now, I think about the factories. It's an incredible process to observe.

it's the game's biggest event, I absolutely love it! I went to Tampa, Florida, for Super Bowl XXXV in 2001 (Ravens versus Giants) and to New Orleans, Louisiana, in 2002 (Patriots versus Rams). The Patriots-Rams game was one of the greatest games I've ever been to in any sport.

I flew down to New Orleans on a Thursday, and when I arrived a limousine was waiting for

Chalk up another pro athlete for the Carolina Blue: Vince Carter and me before the opening ceremonies at the 2000 Olympics in Sydney.

What a game! Here I am in the Superdome in New Orleans after the New England Patriots upset the St. Louis Rams 20–17 in Super Bowl XXXVI.

me. The limo took me to the Sheraton Hotel where I checked into my room. Everyone met in the Gatorade suite before and after events. The suite was beautiful and food and snacks were available at any hour during the day or night. The Fair family would have devastated the spread of food they put out.

Mia Hamm, Kristine Lilly, Cindy Parlow, Julie Foudy, Brandi Chastain, and Bonnie Bernstein (CBS sports reporter) were all there as well, so we hung out a lot during the weekend. We went to a cocktail party the first night, attended the big Gatorade dinner on Friday night, and went to an ESPN party afterwards. I also went to the *Maxim* Models party on Saturday night.

The day of the big game, I woke up at 7 a.m., worked out, ate breakfast, and went to the tailgate party. I have never seen more food in one place in my life. The Barenaked Ladies played before the game.

I went in to get my seat a couple hours early. Security was pretty tight, and I wanted to make sure I didn't miss any of the game. Our seats were great—on the twenty-yard line, three rows up on the second level.

The game was incredible, and we went to the Patriots postgame party afterward. You've never seen a bunch of football players with bigger smiles on their faces. It was, by far, one of the best weekends of my life.

Family and Friends

I think any profession, no matter how enjoyable and exciting, has at least one glitch that can be tough on your personal life. In my career, I travel a lot, which is fantastic, but I'm unable to spend significant time with my family and friends. My teammates are a great second family, but you can't help but miss the people you love.

If I had one wish, it would be to spend more time with Ronnie, Greg, and Pooh. Throughout my life, they have been my best friends, my support system, and my inspiration. Each has been an incredible influence on my life. They have made the difficult times more bearable and the good times even better.

Ronnie Fair

Everyone always asks me what it's like to have a twin sister. I don't know how to answer that because I have no idea what it's like to *not* have a twin sister. I've always been an identical twin, so that's all I know. What I can tell you is that I can't imagine a better way to grow up than having a twin sister, especially when you consider our competitive personalities. If I would say, "Ha ha, I got my hair cut shorter," Ronnie would probably say, "Oh yeah, well mine is longer."

We have so many similarities that extend far beyond physical appearance. But our minds do work a little differently. For example, when we analyze situations, I'm much more logical when encountered with a topic of debate. I take measure of the circumstances and determine right and wrong. Ronnie always seems to find a different angle. She has a very creative mind and has a knack for developing a viewpoint that splits right and wrong down the middle. I guess that's why she's left-handed.

I was so happy when Ronnie was drafted by the New York Power. After spending our collegiate careers on opposite coasts (Ronnie at Stanford and me at UNC), it's great that she's only a train ride from Philadelphia. Whenever something comes up in our lives, we can talk and give each other advice. We're still competitive, but now it's more for each other than against each other.

Greg Fair

My brother, Greg, will always be my big brother. Whenever I do something stupid or make a mistake, I call Ronnie for advice, call Pooh for advice and then say to both of them, "Don't tell Greg!" Seriously, though, he's been a great big brother, but he's been even more than that on many different levels.

Soccer isn't just limited to the Fair girls. Greg played club soccer while he was at the University of California, Berkeley, and currently plays club soccer at the University of Michigan. He's at Michigan earning his master's degree in opera. Greg is an incredible opera singer and will probably begin his career in Europe. I can't wait until the night I attend a show in New York City to watch and listen to my brother perform.

Jennifer "Pooh" Medina

I'm not sure if words can describe how important Pooh has been in my life. She has been my best friend, my training partner, my teammate, and my inspiration. All those nights of additional training after practice that I've talked about, Pooh was always right there next to me. Our hard work on the field culminated with a U-16 national championship playing for the Sunnyvale Roadrunners.

There are a lot of things in life that I'm thankful for, but I've truly been blessed in having Pooh's friendship. Her character is a big part of what makes her so special, and that character was put to the test in high school. A star soccer player with a bright collegiate career ahead of her, Pooh was diagnosed with multiple sclerosis. Many teenage girls would have simply wilted when faced with her condition, but Pooh accepted the challenge and persevered.

With numbness from her chest down to her feet, Pooh had to reteach herself to play the game. Through her unparalleled dedication and commitment, Pooh went on to play four years of Division I soccer for the University of California, Berkley. She is now coaching and runs youth soccer camps.

When there are days that I'm tired or feel like my game just isn't there, I think about Pooh. She has been such an inspiration to me and is a driving force in my life on and off the soccer field.

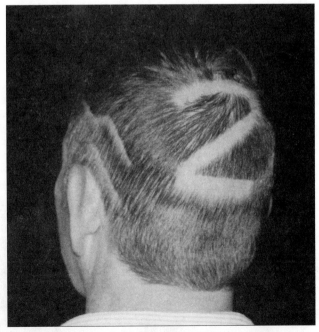

For the 2000 Olympics, crazy Uncle Bob shaved my number 2 in the back of his head. I think everyone has an Uncle Bob in the family.

When the Final Whistle Blows

I'm only twenty-four years old, so I have a lot of soccer left in me. When my passion to pursue something else overtakes my passion to play, then I'll hang up the cleats.

Right now, my other interests are in teaching and possibly broadcasting. I really love kids and feel at home with myself when I'm working with them in clinics. There's a great sense of self-fulfillment when you can make a difference in a child's life. Whatever I end up doing, I think I'll always be working with kids in some capacity.

I've recently been thinking about the prospect of broadcasting. Julie Foudy does it now and Heather Mitts does some college games with the Sunshine Network down in Florida. I'd like to be a color commentator or a reporter down on the sidelines. Obviously, soccer would be a sport for me to cover, but I wouldn't want to be restricted to soccer. I follow a lot of sports, especially football. I grew up loving football, probably because my dad was such a huge fan of those Oakland Raiders. They're all

right, but I love my Niners. I've adopted the Philadelphia Eagles as a favorite, too; now that I'm in Philadelphia, I root for my city's team.

Once I get closer to retiring as an active player, I'll give my post-playing career some more thought. But for right now, I'm doing something that I love. From the time I started playing as a little kid, I've just loved playing soccer. It's taught me so much, brought me experiences I could have only dreamed of, and developed my character as a human being.

My greatest hope in writing this book is that it will help you improve your game and your appreciation for soccer. Remember that soccer is a game, and games are meant for your enjoyment. Focus on having fun, and your passion for pleasure will eventually fuel your motivation to improve and excel. When I started playing, I simply loved having the ball at my feet and taking off with it. And that rudimentary fondness has evolved into an impenetrable affection for the game and a desire to be the best.

I wish you the best of luck with your future endeavors. And when you reach the top, send me an autographed photo. I'll hang it up on my wall with great pride.

A group of us from the U.S. women's national team at Bondi Beach in Australia. I'll never be able to put a price on the experiences I've had and the personal relationships I've developed with my teammates.

An Assessment of Lorrie Fair: The Woman off the Field

"My first impression of Lorrie was a girl who just had this huge grin. She always had the great big smile on her face. I can remember thinking that for a young kid (seventeen years old), she had great charisma. She's just a joy to be around."

—Julie Foudy

"I loved having Lorrie play for me at Carolina, but she's an incredible human being as well. When she opted to stay at UNC for her senior year instead of taking the money she could have earned after the 1999 World Cup title, people caught a glimpse of her incredible value system. I never would have thought any less of her if she didn't return, but it was something she wanted to do. She'll always have a place in my heart for the rest of my life and will always have a bond to UNC."

—Anson Dorrance

"No one is happier to see Lorrie achieve the success that she has than I am. She used to sleep with a little soccer ball every night growing up. The toughest thing is that I don't get to see her as much as I'd like to. We spend time together when she's home (in California), but we used to be inseparable. Every now and then,
I reflect on the past and how great it was growing up with her. I miss those days, but we'll always have a special connection. What she's accomplished has been a dream come true."

—Pooh

"A lot of people look at Lorrie's life with envy. I don't think she'd change a thing, but the truth is, she had to do a lot of growing up very quickly by herself. She made the national team when she was seventeen and was playing among a team of veterans. While we were all finding ourselves and developing our personalities in high school, Lorrie was building her future.

"When we talk or get together, soccer is never a topic of conversation. Our lives are so inundated with soccer that we're much more interested in catching up with what's happening in our personal lives."

—Ronnie Fair

"Both my sisters genuinely care about their friends. They have a vast willingness to do things for other people. Watching Lorrie and Ronnie develop into professional soccer players has been a wonderful experience for me. I've loved every minute of it. It's
something they never considered as a goal growing up. They just loved playing."

—Greg Fair

"One of my proudest moments I had as a mother was when Lorrie decided to go back to school for her senior year and turn down the money earnings from the World Cup. She wanted to finish her education and bring the championship back to Carolina.

"When UNC won the national championship the next year, I went down to the field and gave her a big hug and told her that her dream came true.

"I thought it was an extremely mature decision for a twenty-year-old to make."

—May Fair

"Lorrie always seems to be happy. She's a very positive person. I know she has bad days just like everyone else, but she's able to check her moods at the door. I think that's an important quality as a professional and in an individual's personal life. Her ability to come to practice day in and day out without ever bringing anything personal onto the field is part of what I attribute to her being so successful."

—April Heinrichs

Index

—